The Realistic Therapist

Modesty and Relativism in Therapy and Research

The Realistic Therapist

Modesty and Relativism in Therapy and Research

ROBERT G. RYDER

SAGE PUBLICATIONS
The Publishers of Professional Social Science
Newbury Park   Beverly Hills   London   New Delhi

Copyright © 1987 by Sage Publications, Inc.

For information address:

SAGE Publications, Inc.
2111 West Hillcrest Drive
Newbury Park, California 91320

SAGE Publications Inc.
275 South Beverly Drive
Beverly Hills
California 90212

SAGE Publications Ltd.
28 Banner Street
London EC1Y 8QE
England

SAGE PUBLICATIONS India Pvt. Ltd.
M-32 Market
Greater Kailash I
New Delhi 110 048 India

Printed in the United States of America

Library of Congress Cataloging-in-Publication Data

Main entry under title:

Ryder, Robert G.
  The realistic therapist.

  Includes bibliographical references.
  1. Psychotherapy.   2. Cultural relativism.
I. Title. [DNLM: 1. Psychotherapy. WM 420 R9925r]
RC480.5.R93 1986   616.89'14   86-1765
ISBN 0-8039-2849-1

FIRST PRINTING

CONTENTS

PREFACE

Acknowledging all those who have helped with this work is not easy. The number of people involved is quite large, with any listing bound to slight some, either by a sin of omission or by burying them in a long list. Some people have helped greatly without being aware of the fact. The thoughtful adages I used to hear from Mary Ryder, and her wisdom about the world, have much influenced my thinking. My children have taught me more than they might realize, and one of them will find herself mentioned if she reads carefully enough.

All those who have disturbed my complacency over the years have helped, although it is an open question as to whether they will now prefer thanks or apologies. Like it or not, thanks is what they get. Many people must remain unmentioned, but a few should be named. Reaching back some years, these include John Kafka; and in a very different way, Linda Brandt; and in a still different way, David Olson. More recent additions to this list include Leslie Strong and Carol Love, Kevin Donohue, William Doherty and Robert Ravich, and Sandra Kronsberg. Leslie will find himself the subject of an anecdotal remark if he looks for it, but under another name.

Here in Connecticut, there is a rather lengthy list of colleagues, friends, and graduate students—these several categories overlap quite a bit—who have commented in one way or another, and who have been most helpful. My thanks here include Stephen Anderson, Suzanne Fieldman, Frederick Humphrey, and Ronald Sabatelli, as well as many others.

Particular thanks are due to Cecilia Forgione. She has read and reread, and reread again, offering intelligent criticism gently and patiently.

Colleagues who have had the kindness to offer constructive comments also include Kenneth Gergen and David Kantor. David Kantor has helped both as an individual and as a member of a regularly meeting

7

seminar organized by Donald Bloch and Salvatore Minuchin. I want to thank the organizers of this group and all its members for considering my work. I should be careful to add that my thanks is not intended to imply that everyone actually liked what I have written.

It is customary to thank one's spouse for emotional support and assistance. I would not want it thought that mine is thanked here merely in observance of custom. Jeri Hepworth has richly earned such thanks, many times over. She is also a colleague, and would deserve special thanks were this our only relationship. She has challenged me to think more clearly and to write more simply. Sometimes she has even succeeded. In many ways, she made this work possible.

As one can see, this list includes those I love most, and some known only casually or professionally. To all of them, thank you.

INTRODUCTION

From technique to affection, from fact to commitment. From narrow instrumentalism to a broader, more realistic approach to therapy and research. Realism does not just mean attending to those aspects of the external world that have an unarguable existence. It also means attending to ambiguities, to such phenomena as warmth and tenderness, and to ourselves. It means attending to relativism, used here in the general sense of indicating the extent to which observed reality depends on the location of the observer. It thus means noticing that there are very few things, external or not, that have a genuinely unarguable existence.

Observation is in part an act of creation and hence in a way an act of change. We might then wish not only to observe warmth and tenderness, but to observe with warmth and tenderness. Realism, but not necessarily simple realism, suggests that we adopt an attitude of modesty toward what we can or should do.

It is one thing to notice that there are a number of alternative ways to view the world. In order then to go ahead and view the world, much less do anything else, one must actually choose among the alternatives. Thus the relativism to be considered is one that can look like its opposite, and the modesty is an odd one that urges assertiveness. The intended message is that expanded opportunities for accomplishment are available for social scientists and therapists, if conceptual straightjackets are loosened and self-imposed frustrations are relinquished, and if necessities to choose are faced realistically.

No road map for the future is provided nor shopping list of tasks to be completed. This work is only intended to suggest ways of thinking about tasks, or perhaps it is more accurate to say ways of thinking about thinking about tasks. It is intended, in part, for social scientists who may be troubled by the slow rate of forward motion in social science, for socially oriented therapists who are troubled by impersonal, technique-oriented therapies, and for anyone who is troubled by appeals to objective facts in situations that seem to call for personal and subjective stands. It is also intended for those who value highly most of the work that has been done and is currently being done. For the most part, the suggestions to be made will attempt to trim icons a bit rather than to smash them, and to learn from the past rather than to renounce it.

The emphasis on examples is influenced by my background in the area of marriage and the family, but the main points to be made are more general. They may have some pertinence (not to say impertinence) for anyone concerned with how one can know about human activity, and with how much one can know. Social science and socially oriented therapy refer here primarily to social psychology and clinical psychology, some aspects of sociology, socially as contrasted with chemically oriented psychiatry, and to family studies and family therapy.

Again, one theme of this work is our diminutive size, as professionals, relative to certain tasks that might seem important. A modest attitude toward professional capabilities is advocated, and a realistic appreciation of limits. Some questions may demand answers and yet have no determinate answers. Some goals might seem valuable and yet might best be abandoned or moved to a lower priority. Some ways of achieving goals might be both available and effective but have costs that are too high.

This theme, therefore, expresses a particular point of view. Whether that point of view is idiosyncratic or widely shared in these times is uncertain. Perhaps it is a little bit of each.

A more fundamental theme of this work is point of view itself and its importance. Several sections address this primary theme directly, and others do so by implication.

One repeatedly stated limit is that any understanding of reality, certainly in social science and in the socially oriented therapies, depends unavoidably on the collection of points of view taken by the observer. Personal stands taken by observers are characterized as central, and not as interfering factors to be replaced by the facts. Therefore, in expressing a point of view about limits, the chapters in this book take a particular point of view about point of view.

Other things being equal, the ability to achieve goals depends on the difficulty of the goals attempted. In social science and therapy, the difficulty of goals depends partly on how complex and subtle is the reality to be comprehended and partly on how ambitious is the scientist or therapist. The chapters to come will suggest that it is easy, but unwise, to be tempted by certain unreachable goals. If we aim too high, the projectile we fire might land on our own heads. It might be tempting also, and equally unwise, to redefine reality in ways that make professional tasks seem easier without the tasks actually being easier. When serious human conflict is discussed as if it could be fixed by learning simple verbal skills, or when concepts that hundreds of thinkers have labored over for millennia are defined by a questionnaire of a dozen items, professionals begin to seem like the midwestern state that thought to simplify life by legislating pi to be exactly $3^1/_7$.

It will be argued that modesty and attention to limits, particularly to the centrality of stands taken by observers, are in professionals' self-interest. At least they serve the avowed interests of several relevant professions. If there are choices to be made in how the world is regarded, there is a sense in which acknowledging these choices makes the world better understood. If attempting some tasks accomplishes nothing, it seems likely that taking other directions might accomplish more. If fostering expectations that cannot be met reduces professional credibility, fostering more limited expectations might enhance it. If some vigorous clinical work has costs that outweigh gains, there might be greater benefit in not doing some things.

Several aspects of this work may differ stylistically from what professionals have come to expect. Some apparently simple things are thought to be more complicated than they seem, and the prose reflects this. On the other hand, the style of writing is quite relaxed when it seems appropriate, more so than some may like. It will become clear that adherence to professional forms and procedures for their own sakes is not highly valued here.

One chapter will deal explicitly with values, and how they might best be approached. At that point some arguments will be made relating to openness of values. For now, it may be enough to note that little effort has been made to conceal the values of this author.

Social science and socially oriented therapy have within them many people of imagination, dedication, and competence. They are being joined continuously by new people with fresh ideas. Rather than attempt to tell such people what they should do, this book attempts primarily only to point to some cautions. These cautions are intended to be more liberating than restrictive. Not being able to know something, or noticing that something is not a matter of factual knowledge, does limit the range of one's certainty, but it also opens up the range of one's choices.

With some exceptions, there seems little sense in urging people to concentrate their efforts in some particular direction or other. Some day, perhaps, someone will happen upon the royal road to disciplinary success, making achievements so spectacular that other paths are soon forgotten. In the meantime, it seems preferable to emphasize the broad range of available choices, along with the unavoidable uncertainties and the necessity to choose that are part and parcel of free choice. With a few exceptions, it would be nice if attention to the ideas expressed here led some to branch out into a wider range of directions than might otherwise be attempted.

Greater diversity or not, criticism of some efforts or not, it will be argued that the more overt aspects of professional work (research or therapy) are not usually of paramount importance. There are some exceptions, but generally the ways in which work is regarded, and perhaps the purposes it serves, are of greater importance. As was said earlier, this work is primarily about attitude.

There is some similarity and some difference between the views expressed here and those to be found in other recent commentaries.[1] Few ideas are really new, probably including all of the more basic aspects of the views that will be expressed here. Many readers will find at least some points that seem familiar. However, putting this particular set of ideas in one place, emphasizing the essential unity of the results, and calling them to the attention of those who might be receptive can perhaps have some positive effect.

Note

1. For example, relativism is emphasized here and is also the keystone of Gergen's recent critique of social science (Gergen, 1982). Gergen, however, uses relativism in support of rather different arguments. Gergen's attack on logical empiricism seems most comparable to the chapter in the present work on objectivity and behavior, although his conclusions are more extreme. Gergen almost seems to accept the logical empiricist claim to *be* science, in that he construes an argument against extreme logical empiricism to be tantamount to an argument against all objectivity. Noticing that objectivity depends on the taking of stands that are not themselves objective, he seems to conclude that no objectivity is possible, and turns to a view of social science as a mingling of art and social influence.

I

A VIEW OF THE WOODS

1

A VIEW OF THE WOODS

The trees in this woods are made up of the social science and clinical efforts with which I have had some nodding acquaintanceship in the course of my professional lifetime. I do not plan to list what I have read in my lifetime, or the clinicians I have spoken to, so that an interested person might count or classify these trees. Instead, I mean to step back far enough from the trees that the general outlines of woods begin to take shape and to present some admittedly and necessarily subjective impressions about the woods. The reader is invited also to step back from the trees, at least enough to consider whether the shapes described seem something like reality.

Trees make up woods, but when considered one at a time can easily suggest a view of the woods that is just wrong. One example of such a process is the well-known and even possibly true idea regarding the charts that are sometimes written about long-term patients. Gains are recorded on a regular basis, perhaps for years, but then somehow the patient seems as ill at the end of this process as at the beginning. The Vietnam War is a most celebrated example. During most of the conflict, newspapers carried box-scores of how many people were killed by each side and other information that suggested one success after another. Yet somehow it became apparent that all these successes added up to a monumental failure.

Before getting carried away with examples of positive trees and negative woods, it should be added that I do not believe the social science and therapy woods to have been a smashing failure. I do believe that it has failed dramatically at being a smashing success and that greater success is readily available, particularly for research. To anticipate, I think that a laudable determination to be scientific and to accomplish great things has had some effects opposite to those intended. The apparent weaknesses in research, as I see them, have been greater than those in therapy.

There are thousands of intelligent and competent therapists around the country, even though they vary widely in disciplinary and theoretical allegiances. Although I cannot prove it (and doubt that anyone can), I believe that many people's lives are better because of the existence of these therapists. There are also a certain number of superficial and simplistic therapists at work, who do little good, in my opinion. Unfortunately, the latter group may be composed largely of people trained recently with an orientation to performing easy techniques that are said to lead to quick results. Finally, I think that the administration of therapy, where it is done in agency settings, may have some negative effects on the work that the administration is supposed to support.

As far as research is concerned, while it might be said that the general level of methodological skill is better than it was some years ago, there is still some distance to go. Substantive results that can be depended on, are interesting, and are cumulative, have not been the norm. To switch metaphors, while many people seem to be stepping forward, the army does not seem to be moving very far.

Thus, social science has seemed not enormously successful, although it may have achieved some gains. Psychotherapy has seemed more successful in some ways but may now be changing in the wrong direction, from my point of view. If these views seem too negative, perhaps it should be reiterated that success and failure are not just reflections of actual accomplishments but reflections of relationships between accomplishments and goals. The woods at hand would seem much better if compared to sufficiently modest standards.

For the moment, however, let us take an even more dim view. Let us suppose that the ultimate social goal of social science and the widespread provision of some form of therapylike services is to end or much reduce the severity of at least some social problems. It may be accurate, if not fair, to say that social science has led to the solution of no serious social problem whatever. Similarly, large-scale efforts at providing mental health and counseling services, functional education, and related activities have not produced a noticeable increment in the mental health, marital happiness, or general positive feeling to be found in the population of this country. These same efforts have not produced a noticeable reduction in substance abuse, divorce, violence within the family, or violence and unpleasantness in general.

If subjective impressions are to be trusted, the general ambience of this country is more caught up with violence now than it was when we were actually killing large numbers of people in Southeast Asia. For most of us, life-threatening violence remains something to be found in the media, yet it seems closer to us now than in years past. Films, for example, have changed. Ten years ago, an R-rated film could be counted on to display women's breasts, even if there was no obvious pertinence to the story line. These days there is less nudity, which may or may not be good news. The bad news is that the bodies one does see are more likely to be dead and to have expired on screen in as graphic and novel a way as a creative director can find.

It may be useful to consider some possible objections to this particular dim view of social science and therapy. It might be argued that there have actually been great successes, ignored by me. It might be agreed that society in many regards seems to be in worse shape than it was, but that without contributions from social science and therapy, society would be much worse yet. Finally, it might be suggested that this is a judgment of social science and therapy by totally unrealistic standards. Let us consider these objections one at a time, starting with the view that great successes have actually been achieved.

It might be said, for example, that community mental health centers were set up largely to turn mental health inpatients into outpatients and have mostly succeeded at that. A response to this objection would be that it might be true, but that if it is true, it is irrelevant. The discussion here is about social therapy, and the reduction in mental hospital populations probably has had more to do with politics and developments in chemistry than with developments in counseling (plus the shunting of the elderly to other kinds of institutions). Perhaps some such rejoinder could be noted with regard to other particular successes. Sometimes, however, colleagues say that there are numerous stories of social success but without specifying any particular success. Curiously enough, when specifics are mentioned, they hardly ever seem to be the same specifics. There is no success so noticeable as to command general attention and agreement.

No doubt some successes have occurred (the Headstart program may be an example), but a person could get very old waiting for the evidence that even one serious social problem has actually been brought to an end or has been dramatically reduced as a consequence of social science or therapy.

It might be said that, bad as things may be, they would be a lot worse it it were not for the research and service efforts that have been made. There is no way to refute this argument absolutely, since definitive experimental demonstrations are not in plentiful supply. If plausibility is to be appealed to, instead of unavailable definitive demonstrations, endless argument is possible. There is little to support an unequivocal view that without social science and therapy, as practiced in the last decade or two, the national situation would now be much worse in terms of such things as levels of violence, divorce, or substance abuse.

Another approach might be to agree generally that social science and therapy have not fixed anything major, or even come near doing so, but that expecting them to do so is enormously unfair. Large-scale social trends, it might be said, are massive and complicated things that are not well understood. It would be very simple-minded indeed to imagine that such relatively minor things as social science or therapy could affect them greatly. I agree.

In passing, the fact that major social trends are understood poorly is itself not a big plus for social science. Can anyone recall a major shift in trend that was predicted by some social science establishment? Forgetting entirely about amelioration, few if any social problems are decisively understood, if by "understanding" is meant the ability to make nontrivial predictions of how the problem will change over time.

Suppose then that the cumulative impact of research and therapy has not resolved, or dramatically ameliorated, any serious social problems, but that expecting such an outcome is enormously unrealistic and unfair. How was funding acquired for these research and/or service efforts? Are we to believe, for example, that grant applications were typically written—and funded—in which it was said that if the proposed activity were carried out, it would *not* form part of a structure that would affect any social problem?

Is there a social science establishment, or some psychotherapy establishment, that has made it clear to all—notably including funding agencies—that elimination or great reduction of any social problem is not to be expected as a result of its efforts; not this year, not next year, not ever?

In the early sixties, as I remember them, there was a lot of optimism in Washington. Money was available for worthy causes, and social scientists, among others, were being asked to indicate which causes were worthy. I held a very junior position in the National Institute of Mental Health (NIMH) in the early Kennedy years, and I remember that even I was asked for suggestions about new ways to spend research money. Somebody must have said that social science is not likely to achieve great things simply because it absorbs great amounts of money, but if so, that was a voice not well heard. Someone must have said that he or she was too isolated from the actuality of social problems to be able to prescribe ameliorative policies, but if so, that person's voice seems to have been drowned out by others.

Disenchantment and cynicism were not long in coming. The cute aphorism that there was "a lot of money in poverty," that is, that the poverty programs provided many opportunities for a professional person, was heard too often to be amusing. My impression is that some bureaucrats began to feel "had" before the end of the Johnson years, and that both social science and socially oriented therapy reached a far lower status by the end of the Nixon presidency than they had enjoyed under Kennedy. I am not talking about the views of the politicians in Washington (although one might say that everyone there who survives is a politician to some extent), but about professional bureaucrats who, by and large, continued in office through dramatic changes in national politics.

"Status" is not such a simple matter to assess, and large-scale changes over time are not very well judged by the personal impressions of one former bureaucrat. These impressions are certainly not the whole truth, but they may be a part of the truth. Furthermore, it is possible that one aspect of a decline in the respect accorded social science and related activities has had to do with overselling.

We or our older siblings have claimed too much for our craft, and as one consequence our performance has been disappointing. The disappointment has not been limited to federal funding agencies and has even included some disenchantment within our own ranks.

There are two kinds of consequences of overselling, if it is largely believed by those doing the selling. One kind includes disappointment, reduced status, and other things that might affect future work. The other kind of consequence is more immediate, in that a piece of work may be done in by its own high intentions.

If a researcher sets out to learn whether psychotherapy works, it is imaginable that efforts might be made that accomplish nothing substantive whatsoever, in which case their failure is unaffected by viewing them again later in terms of more modest goals. The same might be said of most research efforts to demonstrate causal connections among nontrivial variables.

If a clinic sets out to treat large numbers of people by limiting any given person to three hours of professional time, come what may, it is possible that the overall "amount" of help, in some sense, may not only be slight, but may be less than the help resulting from an attitude that is less concerned with large numbers. The same might be said of maximizing hours of service delivery by devoting the smallest possible number of hours to supervision, even of junior people. Again, where the overall amount of help provided approaches zero, no amount of re-evaluation with modest goals will turn failure into success. As Yerkes and Dodson (1908) suggested long ago, attempting too much can reduce accomplishment.

Looking again at the woods as a whole, it seems likely that we have hurt ourselves not only by overselling and by some attempts to deliver too much, but also by trying to look too good while we are at it. We have tried too hard to be scientific and to seem scientific. At first glance, such an effort would appear to be invulnerable to criticism. Seeming scientific might be an unworthy intention, but after all, is not the main goal of science to be scientific? Would not therapeutic treatment be improved if based on science?

Let us first address the second of these two questions, since it is less central. Therapeutic treatment might be improved if based on science, or might not be. It depends on how appropriate and successful the science is, and on what the alternatives are to a scientific foundation. Historically, psychotherapy in its numerous forms probably has provided more inspiration to researchers than research has provided to psychotherapists, and there may have been a similar trade deficit in other forms of help. There is no overriding reason to base therapy on research until or unless the research in question can be shown persuasively to be helpful. Whether or not helpful research has actually occurred is really irrelevant. The point is that research in particular, or science in general, has no unique claim to being helpful without having to persuade anyone of its helpfulness. It would even be unscientific to accept science as a basis for therapy without some evidence that this would be a good idea, unless of course science is defined so broadly that the issue reduces to a tautology.

What about the other question: Is not the main goal of science to be scientific? No. The main goals of science are to learn things or to understand them, perhaps to organize and systematize what is learned, perhaps to predict events that have not yet happened, and to learn about things in ways that will not mislead ourselves and others about what has been learned. There may be other and better definitional attributes than these, but the point is that the chief goals of science have got to be the things that a discipline or a particular scientist is out to accomplish. The days when science could be defined in terms of fitting some particular procedural mold have long since passed, if they ever really existed.

Well, one might say being scientific means having these goals and pursuing them in a sensible way. Since these goals are at least among the main goals of science, and since being scientific means having these goals and more, it follows that being scientific is, in effect, the main goal of science. This may or may not be a logical argument. Frankly, I do not much care. The point is one of emphasis. If social science is to accomplish much, an interest in (realistic) accomplishment needs to be more central than an interest in fitting some given role model (even if the role model happens to include being interested in accomplishment).

There are at least four troublesome aspects of the scientific role, as social scientists sometimes seem to perceive it. These are (1) being value free, (2) being quantitative and statistical, (3) building theory, and (4) being—above all—objective. Here as elsewhere in these essays the concern is with excess. Excessive concern with these trappings of science may have negative consequences.

It is obvious that everyone has values, unless of course the point of view is taken that internal states are unknowable and hence either nonexistent or as good as nonexistent. Given the existence of values, they might affect choices of a professional's (therapeutic or research) subject matter—the choice of what is studied, or who is treated. Values might affect the choice of treatment or research modalities—the ways in which treatment or research is pursued. Finally, values might affect goals and hence actual outcomes. What is not obvious is that any of this is necessarily or intrinsically wrong.

We may find it improper to encourage a client to live the sort of life we would like to live, but this is not so much being value free as it is having one value (that clients should lead their own lives as they wish) affect the implementation of others. Another overriding value might be honesty. A third such value, and one to be urged here, is that reasonably clear distinctions be maintained between material that is descriptive and that which is value judgment.

Suppose a person studies a given topic because it is interesting, but says that it is because the topic has scientific importance. The distinction between values and facts is thereby blurred, and a touch of dishonesty is added. Suppose a term is used that claims to be a descriptive label but that seems primarily to express a value judgment about what is labeled. This confusion of facts with values is not likely to be helpful. Suppose a set of factual conclusions is alleged, in which it is implied that something is demonstrated to be better than something else in a general sense. This is another confounding of values and facts.

Attempts at doing totally value free research can slide easily into research that is much involved with values, but in which the values are presented as if they are somehow not values but are matters of descriptive fact.

An analogous situation occurs mundanely in therapy, in which values that are not self-acknowledged by the therapist seem to corrupt the therapeutic work much more than values that the therapist has become aware of. The problem of therapist self-awareness is of course well recognized. The only aspect of it that might be worth noting here, since it overlaps with the research situation, is that the use of diagnostic categories still seems to have some currency as a way to express disguised value judgments of the therapist.

In recent years the psychiatric establishment seems to have decided that homosexuality is no longer a diagnostic category. Are we to conclude that something factual has changed about homosexuality, or are we to infer acknowledgement that diagnostic categories express prevailing social values?

Almost everyone who reads research reports has now and then come across a paper that is totally incomprehensible. Many such papers include elaborate and complicated statistical procedures, described in such a way that outsiders are totally mystified, and insiders (those familiar with the techniques described) cannot figure out the details of what was done. That such papers get published, indeed that on occasion they may get published more easily for being obscure, is testimony to the awe with which complicated statistical operations can be regarded.

Sometimes statistics seem used to create a silk purse from the proverbial sow's ear. A measure, say of marriage satisfaction, is used that consists of one skewed question, or maybe two or three questions are used. This useless measure is applied to a large number of people selected by the best available sampling technique. Nothing need be said about the actual administration procedure, since this is not statistical. The important thing is that a discriminant function analysis is applied to the resulting data because then the results can be published.

Small sample statistics do their own share of harm when used thoughtlessly. Samples of, say, 30 persons do not well represent any infinite population. Yet, the magic attributed to statistical inference is such that this simple fact is readily forgotten if "significance" is obtained.

Many of us seem to have forgotten Mark Twain's view that "there are lies, damn lies, and statistics." We seem instead to believe that statistically expressed facts are automatically more plausible than descriptions put in mere words. Perhaps we might want to give ourselves more permission to draw inferences from what we see and hear directly, rather than just from what we see after it has been "processed" extensively. In some circles there seems to be a law against talking directly to research subjects. If impressionistic material is gathered, permission to mention it in a published report must sometimes be acquired by first providing the reader with an adequate supply of numbers.

Most people would agree that when only waste matter goes into a processor, only waste matter comes out. However, the humblest livestock demonstrate that even when fodder goes in, it can still be waste matter that comes out the other end.

The situation regarding quantitative analyses is analogous to the situation regarding values. Some care to keep values from distorting a research effort is essential, but an effort to appear (or to be) totally and scientifically value free can lead to greater distortion. Similarly, quantitative descriptions are certainly no less desirable than any other kind, and have distinct advantages. Yet, to idolize numbers and to employ statistical inference, no matter how dubious it may be in a given situation, might obscure more than it clarifies.

Theory building has been a popular pastime over the last decade in the field of family studies. Theory for its own sake, somehow as an enterprise that is separate from a concerted effort to learn about a body of phenomena, is not necessarily such a good idea. When data are slight, and findings evanescent, going beyond them to build long (and tedious) propositional inventories can be a distraction from the scientific enterprise rather than its culmination. This is not to belittle all the honest effort that has gone into this work, but it is to suggest that the effort has been misguided. This particular spate of theory building for its own sake will likely come to an end when its course is run, and efforts will be turned to other things. Theory should be the servant of understanding. Turning this relationship upside down—so that understanding is to be used to build theory—can result in vacuous theory and not much understanding.

Again, the point is one of emphasis. There is no intention to urge people to think less, to speculate less, or to be less inclined to spin conceptual webs. Quite the opposite. But when understanding—and anything else available—is to be used to serve the goal of theory building, rather than everything being used ultimately to help understand what is studied, understanding is likely to suffer as a consequence.

The most serious idol to be criticized here is that of objectivity. Perhaps most people think of objectivity as a way of being accurate and certain, and of avoiding bias. No doubt, these are desirable. Less desirably, objectivity can also be used as a way to avoid taking any kind of personal stand. It is not "me" who decides such and such; it is the "facts" that decide. Anyone can see that such and such is (is not) unethical; it is written here in the code of ethics.

Impersonal objective procedures are not very good at dealing with unexpected turns of events, and are not readily applied to subtleties. If objectivity is to be maintained, it may be necessary to ignore subtle and complicated phenomena, or to ignore the aspects of them that are subtle or complex. A single-minded pursuit of objectivity can thus turn into a pursuit of the crass.

Two aspects of clinical work appear to reflect some degree of misplaced objectivity. One is a head count administrative mentality. More people passing through the doors may mean more clinical failure, not more service delivery. The other aspect is the interest in relatively objective aspects of clients' performances, so that rather than help people change, one may teach concrete things such as skills. Some therapists even teach concrete skills by using concrete things they have learned, called *techniques*. Concrete building blocks have their purposes, but their usefulness in psychotherapy may be doubted.

In both research and clinical work, the entire preoccupation with behavior reflects, in my opinion, an excessive insistence on apparent objectivity. In the original arguments for behaviorism, behavior, by definition, is all there is to study (at least in other people). Since nothing else can be studied, all else can be ignored. Well, if everything that can be observed is behavior, there may not be much point in belaboring that fact. If no one *can* observe anything else, no one will. Sin, in other words, is impossible to commit.

Turning the coin over, it may make just as much sense to say that all that each of us can observe is our own phenomenal world. Therefore, phenomenology is all there is to study, and attempts to study anything else are fruitless.

To me at least, it seems pointless to deny that behavior seems to be subject to some kind of organizational system, that is not itself directly observable, whether that system is thought to be intrapersonal, interpersonal, or whatever. Perhaps it is even possible to imagine that an organizational system might change without changes in the incidence of any given behavior, at least as measured objectively, that is, crassly. Perhaps the organizational system might even change in subtle enough ways that observed sequencing among behaviors shows little change. Should organizational changes among a group of entities be regarded as unimportant, or even perhaps as nonexistent, because they do not show in crass observations of the individual entities?

If you ask husbands and wives what is important to them in each other, the answers may start off in terms of behavior but are likely to end in concepts like love and respect—not readily observable behaviors. Many, if not most, clients, if asked what is most important to them about themselves will also come up in due course with statements about so-called internal states. If behavior is thought to refer to externally visible concrete acts, it is usually not as important to most people as attributes that are thought to stand behind behavior, or to organize it, or to give it meaning. Why should we elevate uninterpreted behavior—less important than other things to most of the people we know—to a position of centrality?

The most serious aspect of an excessive belief in objectivity is the view that reality itself is fundamentally objective and that objective reality can somehow be apprehended directly. Suppose it is true that our view of reality, and perhaps in a way even reality itself, depends on choices to be made about where we will stand when we look at it. Suppose, further, that there is no totally objective way to decide where to stand. In that case, reality as a whole, or at least all perceptions of it, depend(s) partly on subjective judgments. Subjective judgments like these are there to be made, they are not trivial, and there is no way to avoid making them. It is possible to imagine that decisions are not being made, simply by imagining that one's own view of reality is the only one or the "obvious" one, but this attitude has costs attached to it. One cost is that discourse with people who believe otherwise gets caught up in foolishness about who is right. More seriously, a limited view of reality might inhibit perceptions that just might be quite interesting, if not useful.

The next few chapters discuss some examples of decision making about views of people. Several dimensions are described, along which implicit or explicit decisions are made about how to regard people or what they do, and it will be argued that none of these decisions can be made on a totally objective basis. There are probably any number of other dimensions that could be described, that would make the same point: Regarding reality as something that can be apprehended in a totally objective way is both incorrect and limiting.

Has overselling mostly come to an end? I think not. As it was with Vietnam, there are just too many places for large claims to be favored over small ones. NIMH seems to have become more insistent than it used to be that some social benefit be linked explicitly to what it supports. Grant writing in general appears to be under more pressure than it used to be to promise highly. Studies that find little (which is most studies) and acknowledge that fact, continue to be disadvantaged in publication.

Attempts to deliver too much, and to be scientific to a fault in so doing, may also be continuing. Of course it is true that the reward system, in funding, in publication, in the academic advancement ladder, seems to support these attempts (if they can be made to seem successful); but external rewards are probably not the whole story. People want to do great and dramatic things, and they want to do many things. Thus they can scuttle themselves by overreaching, and they can scuttle themselves by skimming—by going too fast to do anything really carefully and well.

Modesty, either of purpose or of accomplishment, does not seem to be a central value in our various professions, and it should be. Rumination and speculation, unless "empirically" supported, also seem not to be major efforts that are highly valued, perhaps because they are too humble. Sometimes it seems that thinking itself must be immodestly puffed up and called theorizing, if it is to be well regarded.

We need a breather. We need more mutual support for studying things that are merely interesting, and that might fit together in an interesting way, without trying so hard to be socially useful or scientifically important. If we undertake to help some party change her/his/their life, we need more comfort with our own modest ability to do so in other than crass ways, and more willingness to notice that the therapist's role in therapy is, after all, the secondary one. We might want to encourage in each other and in ourselves more of an interest in the tentative and largely subjective process of learning things about our subject matter, or mutually learning things with our clients, and less of an interest in a "scientific" demonstration that some proposition or other is right or wrong, or that we are clever and effective.

Professional persons in social science and therapy are very resilient and persevere in the face of great odds. These attributes keep one going even after repeated frustrations, but they do not necessarily reduce the frustration. Perhaps a little relaxation would not hurt. They say that some people can run continuously for many miles. True enough; but if people go slowly enough, and rest often enough, they can walk across an entire continent.

Once more, the thesis to be advanced is fundamentally a matter of attitude. Changed practices will not be urged as much as a changed way of looking at what is done, and changes in professional intentions. Alas, the world is more complicated than we would like, and human ability to learn about it, or change it in serious ways, is less than we would like. The old concept of *umweg* seems pertinent. Rather than running vigorously into an immovable wall of obstacles, or pretending that the wall is only a small fence, it might be preferable to saunter a bit in other directions, and not to worry about the wall (important as it might be). Perhaps one of us, while sauntering about and pursuing one interest or another, will happen upon a gate in the wall, and walk through with surprisingly little effort. The odds are that if even a few convincing gates are found, pretty much the entire social science and therapy woods will soon enough work its way through them. If not, well, the odds are too that there is plenty of interesting work to be done on this side of the wall.

II

DECISIONS TO BE MADE

2

DECISIONS TO BE MADE

Jones stands in her home, looking at a clock. The clock is mounted out of doors. In fact, it is mounted on the outside of a missile that has just been launched, and she is looking at it through an extraordinarily powerful telescope. As the missile moves away from her at an ever increasing speed, getting closer and closer to the speed of light, Jones notices a most peculiar phenomenon. The clock that is mounted on the missile appears to be slowing down. Checking this clock against another one by her side, this subjective impression is confirmed: The clock on the missile is slower. Time seems to be going more slowly on the rapidly traveling missile. Is it really?

As I understand this situation, the assertion that time goes by so slowly (or at least more slowly) on the missile in this anecdote requires the existence of several defined factors. There must be two bodies, so that motion can be defined. There must be a clock on each body. Finally, there must be an observer, and the observer must have a defined location. The body on which the observer is located is, by definition, the stationary body. In short, such and such a phenomenon happens, under such and such conditions, *from the point of view* of such and such an observer.

It is imaginable that reality exists and has attributes without regard to any human (or other) observer. It is also imaginable that reality seems different depending on one's point of view. It is not so easy to imagine, but can nonetheless be true, that reality itself, not just appearance, is dependent on point of view. Attributes, aspects, factors of reality—all these exist at a kind of intersection between the world as it may exist unobserved and some real or potential observer. These terms are all descriptions, and descriptions are concepts. They are human (or at least intelligent) creations. If there are no observers, in a real sense there are no attributes. If there are observers, the attributes that exist do depend, in a real sense, on the observers' point of view.

From this point of view (about point of view), there is a response to the old question about whether a tree, falling in the middle of the forest with no one around, makes any noise. Obviously, if noise is defined phenomenologically, the answer is no. If noise is defined in terms of physical vibrations in the air, the answer is yes. The present point is different from either of these. It is simply that if there is no human or intelligent entity in existence to create a definition, to *invent* "noise," the tree makes none. The physical presence or absence of such an entity when the tree is falling is of secondary importance. It only matters if the definition that has been created makes it matter.

Did sexism exist in, say, 1952? Absolutely, from the point of view of the average person of, say, 1980. Absolutely not, there was no such thing, from the point of view of the average person of 1952. What about reality as divorced from any particular point of view? The present point of view (about point of view) is that there is no way to discuss, consider, even imagine reality without taking some point of view. For most if not all practical purposes, there is no such thing as (even barely imagined) reality divorced from any point of view whatsoever. The idea of an unimagined, unconsidered reality is itself a point of view, and it is an idea that shrinks on close consideration. As we imagine what unimagined reality might be like, it is no longer unimagined. It becomes discussable because we adopt a way in our mind of looking at it: We take a point of view.

Note that the discussion of point of view about point of view marks the beginning of an infinite regress. In order to make an assertion about point of view, it is necessary to take a point of view about point of view. Similarly, to make an assertion about this meta-point of view, it would be necessary to adopt a meta-meta-point of view, and so on.

Several distinctions are caught up in a serious way with point of view and touch on this regress. Each such distinction can be regarded as distinguishing among aspects of reality, or as distinguishing among points of view toward an unchanged reality, or somehow as both, depending on one's point of view (about point of view). One such distinction is between variables that are regarded as *contextual* and variables that are regarded as *noncontextual*.

3

INDIVIDUAL VARIABLES
AND THEIR CONTEXT

Hermann is home, glumly looking at a blank piece of paper, and suffering from writer's block. His youngest daughter, age 14 months, comes toddling over, knocks over his bottle of ink, and splashes her hand in it before he can stop her. His middle daughter is 8 years old. She looks at the inkblot and calls it a butterfly. His oldest daughter, age 16, looks at the same mess and says, "Oh look, there are two people kissing." Hermann looks at the inkblot too. What he sees is tenure, an assured career, and perhaps even fame. A test is born.

Two kinds of things happen as the test gradually becomes well known. Many professionals become convinced that major aspects of personality shine out from people's responses to Hermann's inkblots. Furthermore, they see that what is revealed by one or two inkblots tends to be confirmed over and over by the rest of the inkblots in the series, and by other interaction with the testees.

The second development is the growth of interest in scientific quantification. At first, a collection of numbers is coded from responses, and interpretation is based on studying these numbers. After a while, more rigorous procedures are introduced. The code categories become variables that are treated statistically—correlated with each other, correlated with other variables, and used in tests of central tendency. This second line of work comes up with very little. To be exact, no dependable findings of any interest turn up.

Now that science has proven wrong the confidence expressed by test users with less rigor, social scientists gradually lose interest in the test. Without changes in the test per se, could this process have worked out very differently?

Smith and Wesson decide to study the dimensional requirements of home interiors. To be more concrete about it, they want to find out how high doorways have to be if 98% of all adult people in this part of the world are to go through these doorways without ducking. They take height measurements of a large and more or less random sample of people. Person A turns out to be 5 feet 8 inches tall, and so does person B. The computations involving these pieces of information implicitly regard them as identical. That is, not only are the two numbers the same, but their interpretations are the same. They enter computations in the same way, they add or subtract equally from the final, summary statistics, and both A and B count as people who could walk comfortably through a 6 foot doorway.

A and B are the same height, and no other information is needed before drawing that conclusion. Height is used as if it means exactly the same thing for each person measured, without regard for any other characteristics of the person measured, or of the measurement situation, or any other aspects of the context in which the measured height occurs.

The very act of using a number in addition, subtraction, or other mathematical operations expresses the implicit view that (for these purposes) no contextual information is needed in order to explicate the meaning of that number. In the perfect democracy of typical statistical processing, each and every score is subjected to operations according to identical rules without worries about extenuating contextual circumstances affecting a meaning here and there. Variables treated in this way are, in effect, treated as *noncontextual*, as is height in the example just described.

In a study of verbal interaction, person A says something to person B, and then person B laughs and says, "You're a real comedian." A coder working with this bit of interaction duly counts the laugh as one instance of a coded behavior. The investigator listens to a series of taped interactions, and decides that laughter had best not be treated as having the same meaning regardless of context. B might have been responding to a very funny story told by A, or the response might have been closer to that of an innkeeper I refused to pay for my room and from whom I had demanded my deposit back. The investigator therefore regards laughter as a contextually dependent variable, or to be brief, a *contextual* variable, and does not throw all the different laugh codings into a computer to be treated as if they were all equivalent.

Suppose that the investigator decides to recode the interactions and creates a new variable called "Positive Affect." Positive Affect is to be coded on the basis of some set of rules that includes consideration of the previous statement by A. Now that some context has been built into the new variable, the investigator feels more comfortable in regarding the resulting scores as all having similar meaning. In effect, Positive Affect is now regarded as noncontextual. Scores from different occurrences are used equivalently to compute averages, variances, and other statistics and have equivalent effects on the experimentor's ultimate conclusions.

The distinction between contextual and noncontextual seems therefore to be a distinction between kinds of variables; but this is not quite correct.

Some variables, such as height, seem generally to be noncontextual, certainly as compared to amount of laughter; but one can readily imagine a study in which height might be regarded as contextual. In a study of the psychological correlates of height, one might not think that a man five feet eight inches tall is as tall—for the purposes of this study—as a woman who is five feet eight inches tall. Alternatively, laughter could well be regarded as noncontextual in a study of verbal or linguistic styles.

There is plenty of room for argument. The investigator who measured Positive Affect might still, for example, be criticized for considering too little context. Even if Positive Affect really is accepted as a valid measure of positive affect, it might be said that the meaning of positive affect in an interaction cannot really be understood without knowing a great deal about the particular situation in which it occurs and the histories of the interacting persons. According to this criticism, it is an exercise in absurdity simply to take all the affect scores and average them in some way or other.

To summarize, distinctions along the contextuality dimension are neither totally subjective nor totally objective. "Contextual" or "noncontextual" are more felicitous labels for some observations than for others but with plenty of room for observer choice. Decisions along this dimension (or one similar to it) are made implicitly whenever decisions are made as to how data should be treated.

If some variables are regarded similarly by a wide range of investigators, perhaps this has something to do with goals that are widely shared by investigators. Similarly, differences in willingness to exclude or ignore context may have to do with priorities that are different for different investigators. Consider the following, more or less uncontroversial, goals.

It would be nice if research findings replicated dependably with a different sample of subjects, with a different investigator whose ideology is completely different, and with other changes in circumstances. It would be nice if measurements obtained in a particular way related in a meaningful and systematic way to other measures and to measures obtained in widely different settings. It would be nice if what was measured was important in some sense, if it really amounted to something of value to the investigator, to potential consumers of research, to the people studied, to anyone. It would be nice, and this may be one way of indicating importance, if an examination of the measures derived put one in a good position to reconstruct cognitively (or computationally) the raw data from which the measures were derived or a lot of the even more raw events from which the raw data were derived. In one ideal version of this last goal an investigator might meet a subject after studying the subject's scores, and find everything the subject did to be perfectly expectable.

Two kinds of standards are thus described here. One of them has to do with dependability of data, its generality, and the replicability of findings. The other has to do with the importance (or triviality) of measures and findings and particularly with the extent to which something such as an entire person (or dyad, family, etc.) is "captured" by measured data. Allegedly noncontextual variables come into their own in situations where the former set of criteria (dependability, generality, replicability) are paramount.

Within narrow limits, noncontextuality *means* the extent to which measures are thought to be more general than a particular measurement instance, with a particular person or persons, in a unique setting. To be more exact, noncontextuality refers to the extent to which any two instances of a measure have the same meaning for a particular investigative purpose. "Meaning," unfortunately, does not have a very well-defined meaning itself, but at least "same meaning" has as part of its meaning the idea that it is a necessary, if not sufficient, condition for generality of findings.

Suppose that each of 100 subjects has a score for "Tolerance of Ambiguity." For some subjects, the score is a rating provided by teachers. For others, the rating is supplied by subjects' mothers and sometimes by fathers. For still others, the score is computed by summing questionnaire responses based on a scale administered to these subjects. A few subjects have a score from rating themselves. Finally, there is no information at all for a handful of remaining subjects, so they are arbitrarily assigned the overall mean as their score. Many people might agree that in this case it is implausible to regard all pairs of identical scores as having the same meaning, unless of course the meaning in question is junk. Therefore, the variable is not regarded as noncontextual, and it is to be expected that empirical relationships between this variable and a wide range of other variables are likely to turn out to be low, unstable, and strange. Noncontextuality, if viewed as an attribute of variables, does not imply that findings are stable, but its absence does imply instability (in conventional statistical relationships).

Noncontextuality is made more plausible by whatever there is in the measurement process that makes generality more plausible. That is, anything adding to the likelihood that measures will relate cleanly to measures obtained in other situations, and that findings will replicate well, makes noncontextuality a more plausible view. Unfortunately, noncontextuality can be plausible in this sense for very trivial measures. Two questionnaire measures, for example, might relate to each other in a neat and dependable way without either one fitting the second set of standards mentioned above.

Context may well be the key to information that fits this second set of standards, that is, to information that is maximally important, or from which, in a sense, an entire person (dyad, family, etc.) can be reconstructed.

Some investigators may be solely interested in theoretically important variables and care nothing about this second set of standards beyond questions of whether or not the variables in question are well measured. Others may be more interested in the people involved, swallowed whole as it were. Measures designed to suit the interests of this latter group are likely to be better regarded as contextual.

Many years ago I was much embroiled in work with a structured procedure for studying interaction between spouses. The procedure was the Color Matching Test, originally developed by Goodrich and Boomer (1963). In it, spouses were seated on opposite sides of an easel, each looking at a display that consisted of little squares of colored paper. Each square was at least slightly different from every other square, and the squares were arranged according to hue. For example, there was a column of red squares, in which each piece of paper was a different intensity of red, an analogous column of yellow squares, and columns of several other colors. Each square was numbered, so that a person could refer specifically to a particular square of colored paper as, say, "28, Yellow." Finally, neither spouse could see the other spouse's display of colors.

It can be seen that the Color Matching Test was not (still is not, for that matter) the sort of situation that the average person encounters as a matter of normal daily routine. In the testing procedure, a research assistant would hold up a colored square of paper, and ask each spouse to decide, silently, which square it matched of those on the spouse's display. The spouses were then asked to tell each other their decisions and to discuss and resolve any apparent disagreement. This procedure was repeated 20 times, leading to 20 short discussions of which about half usually involved disagreement. Since the husband's display of comparison colors was systematically different from the wife's, it was pretty likely that there would be a substantial number of disagreements.

Coding of Color Matching Test protocols involved a lot of effort to define a set of clear and agreed-on categories into which each statement was placed. Scores usually consisted of percentages of statements in each coding category. Yes, one such score was the percentage of statements in which there was laughter.

Without passing judgment, at least for the moment, as to whether or not the Color Matching Test was altogether a good idea, it can be said that certain procedural aspects seemed appropriate for their purposes. The treatment of data was not very unusual. There was, and still is, nothing idiosyncratic about counting numbers or percentages of statements in various categories and then using the resulting figures as scores. Furthermore, these resulting scores were used, and generally are used, as noncontextual variables. One speaks, for example, of the relative amount of some kind of interactive behavior in families of schizophrenics and families of "normals" or (as I did) of the correlation between "affect" codes and questionnaire scores of marriage satisfaction.

Suppose that a slightly different coding scheme had been used, in which a preceding statement, or even a series of preceding statements, was taken into account in making codings. Other things remaining equal, the resulting scores would have a better case for being regarded as noncontextual, since some context would have been taken into account before the scores were determined. Thus, some spouses might be thought jovial, or others earnest and logical, by virtue of looking at one score or another, but without taking the view (at least for some purposes) that a given score might mean different things for different parties.

How can observational situations be arranged so as to make a noncontextual view of scores as plausible as possible? If one dyad is discussing their first sexual experiences, and another is discussing the difference between bright red and pink, the plausibility of a noncontextual lumping of codes from the two dyads would seem to be reduced.

If one dyad is discussing a difference of opinion that is brand new, just created then, and another dyad is discussing an issue that they have been laboring over for years, this also may make noncontextual treatment less plausible. In general, it makes sense to do all the things that social scientists normally do that keep variations in context to a minimum. One can keep constant the topic(s) of discussion, can try to ensure that disagreements discussed are not (inconsistently) reruns of many earlier discussions, and altogether can keep things simple. Traditional, careful experimental control, in other words, is the watchword. In these terms, the Color Matching Test has some very desirable features.

The downside of careful experimental control is also well known. Well-controlled experimental situations become much more strange as compared to the situations one normally encounters in life. The meaty richness of material that is important to subjects tends to be lost. That is, large (and variable) aspects of context, sacrificed on the altar of experimental control, may affect the meaningfulness and interest of a situation, from the point of view of both experimenters and subjects.

Noncontextual variables may not be the goal of an observational series, or it may be that noncontextual variables are only to be determined at the conclusion of a lengthy inferential process involving much contextual material. Suppose a clinician is approached by a married couple seeking help. For some reason or other it is very important to the clinician to learn quickly whether or not working with this particular couple is likely to be very beneficial (to the couple). Let us not be detained by the question of whether "beneficial" is to be regarded as noncontextual; it is the material acquired on the way to reaching this conclusion that is presently of interest. The odds are that this clinician will not turn to the Color Matching Test.

She or he probably wants to soak up as much contextual material as possible in the hope of better "understanding" the couple. Any questions or other materials presented are likely to be selected so as to provide maximum leeway in which the couple can respond. When some direction of inquiry seems to catch the couple up, all pretense at standardization, or at least much of it, may be dropped to pursue what now seems most interesting. What is probably of most interest to the clinician in this situation, as in others, is precisely the set of connections among different events and aspects of context.

Suppose that the Color Matching Test is being administered and that in the middle of the administration one subject's mother casually strolls into the testing room. From the point of view of an interest in noncontextual variables, a catastrophe has just occurred. A clinician might conclude that this is the only really informative thing in the entire testing session.

From the point of view of contextual material, experimental control is a good way of learning very little. Informative contextual material requires looseness and flexibility. It requires situational aspects that are, or may be, meaningful to some persons studied, but not necessarily to all. So much for the Color Matching Test.

Having one's cake and eating it too is a nice idea, but it is not always possible. If a way of gathering data makes a noncontextual view more plausible, expecting contextual richness in the data is usually inadvisable. If a way of gathering data is suitable for contextual richness, noncontextual variables are likely to be disappointing.

Not paying attention to the difficulties of varying context and holding it constant at the same time can lead to unfortunate efforts to generate contextual and noncontextual data simultaneously or to evaluate data by standards that are unsuitable. Also, the same observations may be regarded differently in different parts of the same analysis.

Studies of observed interaction are sometimes concerned about the statistical reliability of the scores obtained. Typically, agreement between raters or coders is determined in some way and reported, but internal consistency reliability is usually ignored. Generally, internal consistency should be computed. If a variable is thought to be related to aspects of a person or dyad (or whatever) that might also be found outside of the testing situation, it is only sensible to expect it to be related to itself, that is, to the same variable as measured elsewhere in the same testing situation.

The response that I have received most often to this view is that internal consistency reliability would be inappropriate because different portions of an experimental interaction situation are not equivalent to each other. Interaction, for example, on Trial 1 cannot be compared meaningfully with interaction on Trial 3 because different topics are being discussed, because the level of stress is different, fatigue factors are different, and so on. In short, this response implicitly characterizes the interaction scores from each trial as contextual. The trouble is that this contextual view of variables is directly contradicted by subsequent treatment of the same variables.

The typical study of observed interaction does not compute internal consistency reliability, for the reasons mentioned earlier or for some others, but then goes on to treat scores as noncontextual. They are summed or averaged in some way over trials and/or otherwise used equivalently to each other in a variety of other statistical operations.

One cannot readily have it both ways. To be more exact, one cannot have it both ways without what amounts to logical sleight of hand.

It is always possible that there are other, quite good reasons for regarding internal consistency reliability as inappropriate. It is also possible that internal consistency reliability may be avoided for inappropriate reasons not related to contextuality. For example, there may be some inchoate suspicion that internal consistency reliability, if computed, will turn out to be very low. The point here is only that the situation is not helped by a lack of conceptual clarity about contextuality or some similar concept. If two trials are so different that consistancy among them should not even be measured, it seems a bit odd to regard them as similar enough to be pooled in computing summary statistics.

Unfortunately, there seems to be a widespread temptation in the social sciences to attempt more than can be accomplished. It would be nice if one neatly packageable procedure yielded beautiful noncontextual variables and at the same time provided the contextual richness that would seem fully revealing about the relationships and the lives of those studied. It is unlikely that this goal can be achieved.

The quixotic attempt to provide fully contextual substance and cleanly noncontextual variables at the same time can be very expensive. The greatest cost is not because such a research effort fails, but because it seems falsely to succeed.

Almost anyone can score a large number of variables from highly contextual material such as dialogue, written essays, or nonverbal behavior. Since coding may be cheaper than testing, there may be even more codes than there are independent observations. At least there may be a great many codes. Under these circumstances, the odds are high that something interesting will turn up in the data, but the odds are low that the same interesting thing will turn up again if the study is replicated. The problem of analyzing an excessive number of correlated variables is well known, but has not gone away, and seems particularly pertinent to the analysis of variables coded from highly contextual materials.

The use of allegedly noncontextual variables drawn from highly contextual material such as dialogue, written essays, or nonverbal misleading. Suppose one collects such materials from two somewhat different groups of persons (neurotics and psychotics, Irish and Italians, people who grew up with two parents in the home and people who did not). Suppose further that, say, a sample of personal letters is acquired from each person (from which obvious references to diagnostic status, ethnicity, and so forth, have been expurgated). The investigator then acquires the services of the most perceptive clinician in the country, who proceeds to code a variety of (allegedly) noncontextual variables. Lo and behold, some combinations of these variables do distinguish between the groups in question. The clinician had been told what groups were to be distinguished but had no advance idea of which letters were written by representatives of which group. The clinician also had some theoretical ideas about the kinds of variables that might differentiate the groups in question and constructed codes that were intended to tap these variables.

It may be true that these variables, coded by this clinician in these circumstances, do differentiate between groups. The issue is, is the differentiation due primarily to the circumstances, to the choice of coded variables, or to the choice of clinician? It is entirely possible that the clinician reads a person's letters, comes to some feeling (perhaps not even consciously) about which group they come from, and then codes a set of variables. The variable coding could then be guided, subtly and perhaps unconsciously, by contextual factors that appear nowhere in the variables' written definitions. If this possibility or something like it occurs, a consumer of the research would be much misled if the research were interpreted to mean either (1) quantitative support for the theoretical variables thought important by the clinician or (2) support for the usefulness of a particular set of noncontextual variables coded from personal letters.

Tailoring a procedure carefully so as to yield defensibly noncontextual variables brings its own problems. It may be that in some studies of observed interaction, and perhaps in some other kinds of investigations as well, there is no way at all to create plausible noncontextual variables without so trivializing the remaining data as to eliminate any serious justification for doing the research. It does not wash to argue that such and such a code is used because, in the current state of the art, "It is the best we can do," if the best available is still trivial. It might be better, in such a dreary circumstance, to let go of the project that has turned out to be impossible to do in a meaningful way and to do something else instead.

So far, this discussion has been put as if there was a close correspondence between the contextuality distinction and a distinction between clinical and nonclinical. The two distinctions are certainly related but are not equivalent. The contextuality distinction is applicable in work that has no clinical purpose and even in "strictly" quantitative studies. It may make perfect sense to regard two identical questionnaire scores, for example, as meaning the same thing, or it may not. "Measuring context" might refer to a subjective clinical judgment, or it might mean a computational procedure in which the interpretation of some quantitative data was made dependent on other quantitative data. Historically speaking, the most careful consideration of context is probably not by clinicians at all but by experimentalists.

Perhaps, even within the arena of strictly quantitative data, there are ways to generate better noncontextual variables from situations that have not been actually controlled to death. One might try to measure context in some way and take it into account in constructing noncontextual variables. An example of such a procedure has been mentioned, namely the possibility of defining an interaction variable in terms not only of what is being said but also in terms of what has been said previously. Alternatively, interaction sequences as a whole could be coded or characterized by scores derived from sequential information within the sequences. Even questionnaire scores might be improved if made conditional on some measurable aspect of context.

No solution or even amelioration comes without its own problems. In this case, there is the small problem of obtaining noncontextual measures of context. Measuring context in order to refine variables may be not much easier than measuring the original variables. Furthermore, some statistical properties of the scored variables, such as reliability or skew, could get dramatically worse as scoring becomes more complicated. Still, if context really cannot be eliminated as a serious source of variability without eliminating what one wants to study, measuring context in some way would seem to be a strategy that should be tried.

Many people still believe that the Rorschach test yields clinically important information, but there is perhaps some realistic doubt as to whether the large number of quantitative Rorschach studies that used to be so popular generated much in the way of solid and repeatable substantive findings. Using the Rorschach with an entire family may also be useful, perhaps even very much so, but perhaps it is overly daring to regard interaction variables coded from a family Rorschach administration as noncontextual. If so, then what might have happened differently (in the fable that began this section), that might not have concluded with such a dismissal of Hermann's inkblots? Was this process merely a matter of correcting misguided enthusiasm or of technical shortcomings either by the less rigorous professionals or by those with more scientific rigor? The social scientists made an error and did not make an error. Given their implicit assumptions and frame of reference, they made no error. Some qualifications might be added concerning the technical state of the research art, but the technical state of the research art can to some extent be viewed as a consequence of assumptions and frame of reference. The error, if there is one, may be in not noticing that the social scientists' conclusion is contingent upon particular assumptions and/or points of view. It may not so much contradict the other professionals' work, as be irrelevant to it, or even provide support for a very different conclusion— that the point of view adopted by the social scientists is a not very productive one for this situation.

The social scientists, at least in this anecdote, have tended to take the methods and assumptions of traditional social science for granted, and to use these to evaluate, that is, to pass judgment on, such things as clinical procedures. Anticipating a point to be made much later, suppose another set of intentions was more prominent. Suppose the judgments and perceptions of, for example, clinicians were taken as given. Would the conclusions then be some evaluation of social science methods? Suppose evaluation itself were not so important, and the chief goal were "merely" to express and describe the "naive" insights of the less rigorous professionals, perhaps in quantitative terms. Would this have been of earthshaking importance? Probably not. It might have been mildly interesting. It might have spurred on some quantitative developments not otherwise imagined, because otherwise they would not be very pertinent. Results might even have included some instructive information or ways of thinking that would be informative about how people see, or feel, or are.

Dropping for now such fuzzy-headed meanderings, the point to be most emphasized is that whether one is a clinician or not, the variables one uses and how they are used should depend on the full matrix of one's purposes, one's conceptual view of what is being studied, and on a thoughtful view of the circumstances in which measurement is to take place. Being clear about contextuality is, in my opinion, a reasonable part of this thoughtful view.

4

INDIVIDUAL PEOPLE AND THEIR SYSTEMS

Counting seems like such a straightforward matter that it may not appear to be more than merely a technical problem. One decides what to count and then does so. The major problem of course is in deciding what to count, unless it is people who are the objects of this procedure. Then it seems natural that individual persons should be the unit of analysis, so that one person counts as one, two persons as two, and so on. It is pretty trite by now to suggest that an alternative counting process might be preferable in which the counting goes from one person to one dyad to perhaps one family. Let us ignore labels that refer to still larger groups, at least for now.

Studying or treating individuals, considered as such, has an attractive simplicity to it. An individually oriented therapist can be devoted to relating everything that happens in therapy to an understanding of one given individual and/or helping that individual to change. Researchers can describe samples on the basis of how many individual persons are in them, can measure individual differences, and can generate conclusions about the nature of people, taken one at a time.

It is almost as easy to take a different attitude and regard it as the only correct one. Reasons of professional affiliation or ideological conviction might result in the belief, say, that the family is the only correct object of professional attention. One difficulty with this second attitude is that implementing it may not be as easy as taking it. The question of what it means to treat a family has answers that vary in permissiveness. At the more permissive extreme, if a therapist has only two people in the room (the therapist and a client), but intends the client's family to be the object of therapy, what is going on can be regarded as family therapy. At the less permissive extreme, a therapist can have an "entire" family in the room but be concerned only with one person (or only one person at a time) and not be thought of as really doing family therapy.

A family-oriented researcher may want to study families but may use variables that others regard as only referring to individuals. The exclusive use of variables that everyone will regard as referring to larger than individual units may be thought difficult to accomplish without sacrificing information that the researcher finds to be important. Either a therapist or a researcher may thus intend a family orientation, but may or may not be able to convince all coreligionists that the intention is actually carried out. More or less the same set of generalizations applies to a dyadic orientation and perhaps to others as well.

One way to take an individual orientation is by means of not noticing that other attitudes are available. The problem of choice does not arise, at least not phenomenologically, if only one alternative is seen. If more than one choice is seen, but only one is believed to be correct, the problem of choice arises but has an easy solution (passing over problems of implementation). One other way to avoid actually having to choose is to see alternatives but to try taking them all simultaneously or to shuffle back and forth among alternatives rapidly enough so that they might as well be simultaneous. Clinicians of a certain theoretical persuasion might recognize these ways of avoiding decision making as going from a pattern that is like hysteria (not seeing alternatives) to one that is like obsessionality (trying somehow to go all ways at once).

A researcher might adopt some grand systemic synthesis in which everything from subatomic particles to the universe as a whole is organized into a multilayered, multidimensional space, complete with suggestions about interfaces among the layers. With or without such a grand design, one might study individual variables, dyadic variables, and family variables, and thus leave nothing (?) out. Why not?

There is certainly nothing intrinsically wrong with classifying a set of variables into subsets called individual, dyadic, or something else. Whether or not it is a good idea to do so in some particular instance depends, obviously, on the circumstances. Suppose, however, that the investigator in question imagines that the classification process has avoided the necessity of choosing among individual, dyadic, or other orientations. It has not. To imagine that choice has been avoided usually means, here as elsewhere, that choices have been made without paying much attention to them.

It is tempting to regard these different ways of dealing with choice as progressions in sophistication. Sophistication sometimes, perhaps often, seems like a circular process if regarded casually. There is a position that is regarded as most innocent or naive. Other positions, as they become more and more sophisticated, are more and more different from this original position. Beyond some point in sophistication, the most sophisticated positions seem somehow to be similar again to those that are the least sophisticated. For example, it is naive to believe that the other planets and the sun revolve around the Earth. A more sophisticated position is that the Earth and all the other planets revolve around the sun. Getting more sophisticated yet, it can be said that maybe the sun does revolve around the Earth after all. It depends on one's point of view.

Similarly, naive people believe that behavior is only part of what is interesting and important about people and might be quite interested in each other's internal states. A more sophisticated "behavioral scientist" might point out that behavior is all there is to be observed, and that therefore only behavior is important to study or to treat. We will omit for the moment an opinion of what a person might believe if that person were still more sophisticated.

Applying this alleged cycle of sophistication to the matter at hand, the most naive approach is to see only one alternative. If an observer imagines, say, that the world is populated only by individuals, the problem of choice does not arise. While this approach is blind to other possibilities, it can be coherent and more or less self-consistent.

It is arguably more sophisticated to believe that a family (or a dyadic) focus is the only correct one. This approach does at least notice the existence of more than one possible orientation. Its innocence is in believing that only one is correct, or most correct, more or less in general. Believing that one orientation is the only correct one is likely to involve the belief that there is a correct definition of that orientation, and that that definition refers somehow to reality, to something "out there." When reality turns out to be slippery, the going can get a little messy.

It could be said that still more sophistication is involved in perceiving several alternatives and believing that all might have value. Variables are then classified as, say, individual, dyadic, or other, to pay some attention to each alternative. If it is imagined that this process avoids having to choose among possible alternatives, notably for any given variable, then this position also may be accused of some naiveté.

Pursuing these allegations of sophistication still further, and only considering one more position, maybe the most sophisticated position (of those described) would be like the least. An investigator with such a position might be well aware of the possibilities of individual, dyadic, family, or other orientations, but might find it of interest to take one orientation as a stand, to act *as if* only one of these points of view existed, at least at any given time. Here a certain tolerance for ambiguity and paradox is needed and acceptance of more than one logical level. It is necessary to imagine not only multiple points of view but to imagine multiple ways of dealing with the multiple points of view.

Supposing that an organization of these positions in terms of sophistication has some merit, it should be added that any such organization might well be taken with some salt. If it is pushed further, we come to two distressing observations. First, it is reckless to believe that any given position is "most" sophisticated, particularly if the position in question is intuitively appealing to the person doing the judging. Second, the question of what is more or less sophisticated has got to be a matter about which there can be several points of view, perhaps even points of view that differ in—what else?—levels of sophistication. Let us move on.

Considering individual, dyadic, family, and possibly other orientations, the argument here as elsewhere is it may be impossible to avoid choosing one point of view and in so doing to turn one's back on other possible points of view, at least at any given time, with regard to almost any given aspect of the people observed.

A particular behavior, X, occurs. An observer records the occurrence and nonoccurrence of this behavior in some setting and thus turns it into a quantitative variable. Very few people are likely to be much interested in X without knowing what it is. What does that mean? It must mean, at least, that one knows something of the measurement operations, something of the content of the behavior being treated this way, and something about who enacted the behavior. It seems likely that even if an investigator claimed only to be interested in particular variables, and not much in the people standing behind them, the investigator would still want to know this much.

If it turns out that Sam Samson enacted the behavior in question, we might conclude that the variable pertains to him. Since Sam is an individual, we could add that this is an individual variable. To generalize slightly, a variable can be classified on the basis of its *author*. Sam did it, so the coded material is Sam's score, and since Sam is an individual, the variable X is an individual variable.

It only takes a moment's reflection to see that this view may not be so easy to apply in all cases. Suppose X refers to Sam's assertion of something or other about his wife. Can we still say that X is Sam's score, or might we have some inclination to treat it as Sam's wife's score? Do we still regard it as an individual variable, or might we feel that perhaps something dyadic is going on here? Similarly, if X is Sam's report of general family satisfaction in his family, how is that report to be regarded? Finally, if content is not attended to, is it meaningful to speak of any behavior as referring to dyads or families? Is it not true that all behavior is emitted by individuals?

Setting Sam to one side, and turning away from research altogether, let us consider observation as it might sometimes occur in a therapist's consulting room. Unless treatment has developed some odd new wrinkles, there will be N people in this room when therapy is in progress, with N being never smaller than two. For convenience, let us suppose that there are actually three or more persons in the room, of whom two or more are clients. A therapist has at least three choices as to what he or she looks at and sees. First, the therapist can attend to what some individual is doing, and "see" individual behavior, that is, the therapist can imagine the activity to reflect something, well, individual, about this person. Second, the therapist can somehow perceptually capture the collection of individuals in interaction (perhaps even including the therapist). The therapist sees and hears several persons doing things with and to each other and may attempt some perceptual disentanglement of the complete network of interactional influence and information transmission. This second stance is in a sense a middling one in that much of what is going on between the participants is organized in some way (in the therapist's perceptions or cognitions), and yet what the therapist sees is individual persons, perhaps with individual feelings and wants, who are engaged in interaction.

The therapist's third choice is to look out at the room and see (hear, feel, etc.) only one animal ("us"), or perhaps two ("them" and "me"). This choice seems to be fundamentally a phenomenological one in that a dyad (even a patient therapist dyad), or a family, is actually experienced as a kind of "multipede"—a beast with many legs but only one head. This almost perceptual experience may come and go, perhaps depending partly on "individual" characteristics of the therapist. In any case, it is not possible to experience a group of people in this way and at the same moment to experience them as a collection of interacting individuals, much less as one individual plus background.

Anyone who has read *Gödel, Escher, and Bach* (Hofstader, 1980) will remember how easy it was, in the context of fictional anecdotes, to see

Aunty Hill as a moderately intelligent, single character, even though she was really an ant hill. Aunty Hill was logically distinct from the ants out of which she was built. It is fair to add that perceiving her, like our therapist's perception of the multipede in the consulting room, was also phenomenologically inconsistent with clearly "seeing" the individual ants.

Regarding several people as one creature is not simply a phenomenological oddity. It has a few ramifications. The primary pertinent aspect of most entities that are seen as one living being with a modicum of intelligence is that such a being has many modalities available for carrying out actions, but basically there is only one "executive" (brain, intelligence, personality, or other similar term) for whom things are carried out. While the beast may have many "legs" (modalities of behavior), it has only one "head" (organized system of executive functions). The "head" appears to hang in the space among the participant persons, which is appropriate, since it *is* the organization among them.

A therapist who is dealing with the multipede (at some given time) regards anything nominally done by any individual as actually an act by the larger animal. If an intentionality orientation is being adopted, anything nominally done by anyone is thought of, and may be responded to, as if it expresses the wishes of this corporate entity. If the therapist includes him or herself as part of the entity, even the actions of the therapist might be regarded—at that moment—as expressions of the beast. This is not the same as suggesting that any one person's actions express the wishes of all, because such a suggestion seems to imply some consensus among group members. It is quite possible that no one group member is aware of having intentions that seem crassly visible—even to group members—for the group thought of as one entity.

The therapist's three ways of seeing those in the consulting room are paralleled by three ways of regarding the authorship, as it were, of any act. The act can be thought of as expressing (coming from) an individual, reflecting individual characteristics only. It can be thought of as coming from the individual in some social context (and here the context need not be restricted to persons physically present). Last, it can be thought of as being "authored" by a dyad or family, or other group.

One other alternative that seems attractive, at least at first glance, is that any action be thought of as expressing partly individual and partly supra-individual characteristics. There is an analogy here to the business of classifying variables into subsets (individual, dyadic, family, or other). That is, there is no reason for objecting to variance being divided, conceptually or otherwise, into portions due to different sources. The argument is only that what has been said about variables is then applicable to portions of variance. There is no way to avoid deciding—based on some implicit or explicit conceptual position, or willy nilly—that a particular overt act, or aspect of an act, or portion of variance of the act, is authored by one or another parties, such as individuals, dyads, or families. A close examination of the basis for making such a decision is likely to reveal that the choice is not totally a matter of logical necessity, that is, that the chooser cannot so easily be extricated from the decision process.

If an observer's view is that everything people do is, by definition, individual, then the question of defining "individual" is made easier. There is no need to worry about how one kind of behavior can be distinguished from another. If one kind of act (or aspect of an act, or portion of variance) is to be regarded as individual, and another kind as being, say, social (either because some social entity is said to be its author, or because an individual enacting the behavior is thought to be influenced by some social context), then there are complications.

If Sam does X only in a particular social context, it would seem reasonable to call X social. But what if Joe never does X in that setting? If nonindividual characteristics are to be characteristics that depend on (vary with?) social context, what is an individual characteristic? If it is a characteristic that is displayed in situations absolutely without a social context, it is quite forgettable. If it is a characteristic that is displayed in the "average" social context, a decision-making problem has apparently been solved but at the expense of creating a problem that is unsolvable. The prospect of defining a universe of all possible social contexts, sampling from them in some meaningful and random way, and exposing any given person to this random sample of situations, is nil. It is of course feasible to define a very restricted universe of social contexts, for example, face-to-face discussion of a given topic with each of ten particular people. But if this last option is selected, it should be recognized that a quite restrictive definition of "individual" has been made. There may be plenty of other contexts in which the allegedly individual attributes, found in an experimental implementation of this definition, seem not to exist.

One could also go for a definition based on limits. At one extreme, anything a person does in any situation (for example, in the context of the ten people mentioned above) could be counted as individual. But this is just saying that everything is individual. At the other extreme, characteristics might be regarded as individual only if they seem (by means of something at least potentially observable) to be present in all situations. Nothing can ever be proven individual by this decision process, since we are faced again with the impossibility of getting even a random sample of all situations. Of course, many things might be proven nonindividual, since this latter alternative only requires one observed situation in which the characteristic does not appear.

Let us put some flesh on the business of Sam and his behavior, X. Sam is at a cocktail party interacting with the other guests, among whom are some women he finds attractive. X refers to some aspect of the way he interacts with these women. Inconvenient as it may be for social science, the social context that is most pertinent here may not be that of the cocktail party alone. It may include at least one person not physically present—Sam's wife. It is quite imaginable that what Sam does is strongly influenced by a social context that includes the fact that he has a wife and that also includes some salient facts about the kind of marriage he has and the kind of individual his wife is (in the context of her marriage to Sam).

What is to be done with this example of Sam, in which the social context under consideration is one that Sam is *always* in? There is no obvious way that marriage and family contexts, not to mention others that people carry around with them, are subject to any of the experimental manipulations envisaged above.

The point of emphasizing complications in ways of classifying characteristics is not to show that classification is necessarily a bad idea. It is only to show that most if not all schemes for doing so depend ultimately on stands taken by an observer. Choices must be made that are neither self-evident nor required by the nature of things. For almost any characteristic, an observer cannot avoid choosing an individual or some social point of view and in so doing is preempted from taking another point of view at that time.

Different points of view taken toward the same body of data can be virtually opposite to each other. In a family orientation, everything that Jane does, and all the attributes that superficially seem to pertain to Jane, may be regarded as information about Jane's family and contribute (along with information from other family members) to generalizations about the family. If an observer is oriented to Jane as an individual, information from all family members, perhaps exactly the same information, may be used in order to learn more about Jane. For example, it might be suggested that Jane's choice of spouse says something about her intentionality. Hence, information superficially attributable to the spouse can be used to fill out the picture being derived of Jane. Similarly, it can be said that the characteristics of the children must reflect, to some degree or other, Jane's intentions (verbalized and other) and practices. If you want to see what a person is really like, it might be said, look at the person's children.

Information apparently derived from any family member can be thought of as an expression of a family as a whole, and information from a family as a whole can be regarded, perhaps with profit, as informative about some given family member.

Here is a recapitulation of the argument so far. Human characteristics can be regarded as individual, or as dyadic, family, or other. The general term settled on to mean nonindividual has been social.

Emphasis has been placed here on social groupings that "naturally" occur in life rather than some collection of people put together after they have been individually and randomly sampled. The experimental manipulations suggested apply only to ad hoc groups, but otherwise much of what has been said seems to apply to both kinds of groups.

It has been said that regarding a variable as individual or social depends usually on who or what is thought to have emitted the behavior that an investigator codes, or (if the behavior has informational content) who or what the informational content refers to. The discussion here has emphasized who or what has emitted the behavior, in referring to "authorship," to keep matters slightly more simple. If both authorship and referent of behavior are to be considered, a new set of questions arises as to who is observed and who is observer. That is, one conclusion might arise if Joe's report about Sally is to be observed, and another if Joe is to be regarded as an observer of Sally. A third basis for regarding a variable as individual or social is whether or not it is regarded as, or can be shown to be, a function of social context. In this case, Joe's report about Sally might be regarded as pertaining to Joe as an individual but only in a context that includes Sally.

It has been said that one can regard a group of people, perhaps even including oneself, as one corporate entity. Hence, one can regard anything that seems (superficially) to be done by any group member as actually having been authored by the group. In effect, it has been argued also that even though imagining the existence of a multipede may seem a little crazy, there is no obvious reason to rule it out. At the least, it might be heuristic as a point of view, either in therapy or in research.

While group-authored behavior may not be as crazy an idea as it might seem, individual authorship that does not reflect a social context may not be quite as easy to define as it might seem. Either way, decisions must be made and must be made on the basis of some stand taken by the observer, whether that stand is taken knowingly or not. No stand is seen readily as a matter of logical necessity. Finally, stands appear to be mutually exclusive of each other as applied to the same thing at the same time.

There are some variables that only exist for groups or for groups of certain-size characteristics. There can be no question that group size, for instance, is itself a variable that does not vary if applied either to individuals or to dyads. Coalition formation is difficult to imagine in groups of less than three. These are commonplace observations, however, that apply only to a narrow range of variables.

Whether a variable or some portion of it pertains to individuals, dyads, or families is nearly always a matter of how an investigator chooses to regard it. Some variables may more popularly be regarded in one way and others in some other way, since this distinction, like the other distinctions discussed in this group of essays, is not totally a matter of subjectivity, but the variable that cannot be viewed in more than one way is extremely rare. To say it another way, the distinction between individual variables and one sort or other of social variables is less a matter of what is "out there" in the variables than it is of what is "in here" in the point of view of the observer.

Virtually all so-called individual variables can also be regarded as dyadic or familial. All so-called dyadic variables can also be regarded as familial. Finally, there is no reason to believe that familial variables cannot be regarded, maybe with some profit, as "actually" being attributes of some still more inclusive grouping.

Not only must an observer, in effect, make choices along these lines, there is no present way to know which choices will lead to the most interesting generalizations. The general purpose here, as in the other essays in this section, is to urge attention to this fact. Movement in any given direction is likely to involve giving up some freedom to go in other directions, and choices nonetheless must be made without clear knowledge of where they will lead.

The essays in this section have been put largely in terms of choices among different points of view from which some relatively fixed set of things could be observed, whether the observation is for research, for therapy, or somehow for both. The things under consideration have been described as aspects of people, attributes, behaviors or actions, or as variables. In the present essay, mention has even been made of aspects of aspects in the discussion of classifying portions of a variable's variance. However, the focus might be shifted in several ways. Perhaps it is not necessary to regard variables, behaviors, or even aspects of behavior as such, as the primary objects of attention.

If an observer is clear that she or he is primarily interested in individual people, dyads, families, or whatever, choosing an individual, dyadic, or other interpretation of actual data should be easier.

If an observer is clear about which aspects of people or groups are of interest, and which are not, decision making leading to plausibly noncontextual variables might be facilitated. It is possible, of course, that instead of being interested in a few variables or a few hypothetical constructs, an observer goes to the opposite extreme and wants to understand individuals and/or groups more or less in their entirety. In such a case it might be that no actual data could be regarded as noncontextual, with consequences that might be interesting, but that also might be fatal to any inquiry whatsoever.

There are two points here. One is the general thesis that observers must and do make many decisions that narrow the scope of their work and that inevitably leave things out. Usually, more so than may be realized, these decisions are nonrational in the sense that they are not given by "the nature of things," or by some *ex cathedra* statistical operation, or by an objective calculation of costs and gains. They are a personal matter for the observer. The second point is that choices may be a lot easier for an observer who is clear about her or his interests, than, say, for a person who claims scientific impartiality or who is evenly and blandly interested in everything.

Given the choices to be made, is there a better way to make them than on the basis of personal interest?

In the case of research, "scientific importance" might be thought of as a better guide, but perhaps we might hesitate to follow it until someone defines "scientific importance" in a persuasive way that applies unambiguously and consensually to social science. Usefulness for social good is another possible standard, but definitional ambiguities to one side, the track record of social science suggests that this standard calls us to attempt achievements that are not realistically available.

In the case of therapy, the choice of focus ought to be simple enough, based primarily on what works best. Unfortunately, this idea turns out to be more simple-minded than simple. First, "works" is a term for which therapists of different interests have different definitions. Second, therapist values, if not client values, set some limits on modalities regardless of effectiveness issues. Third, even if the first two problems can be resolved, no one should lose sleep waiting for convincing evidence that one form of therapy is "better" than another within the range of contemporary "talking" therapies as applied to people not in captivity.

There are exceptions and quibbles applicable to these generalizations, but by and large the question is not whether we as observers *should* make choices mostly on the basis of our personal (dyadic, familial?) interests. Some day, someone or some group may catch a brass ring—may achieve the kind of investigative or healing triumph that converts everyone to one set of interests. In the meantime, we *will* be guided primarily by our own varying interests. "Interest" as expressed by people who have spent a lifetime being concerned with studying or treating people is perhaps not such a frivolous thing. Perhaps we should trust our interests more, do the same for each other's interests, and in general regard interest with more respect. "Interest" as compared to such expressions as "scientific importance" at least sounds a little more modest and a little less pretentious.

5

SUBSTRATE VERSUS INTENTIONALITY

All across the country there are programs and academic departments called human development and family relations, or child and family studies, or some similar name. Sometimes the two elements have been put hierarchically, as in the erstwhile Child Research Branch of the National Institute of Mental Health, in which the Family Development Section (where I worked) was located. Sometimes there is a third component, as in a department of family and community studies, and now and then family and individual development are separated administratively.

Primarily, though, someone seems regularly to have thought that individual development is close enough topically to studies of marriage and the family that the two should cohabit, although long experience has shown that a real marriage between the two topical areas (at least in the culinary sense) is unusual. That is, the two areas have rarely blended together to form a new and cohesive organic whole in spite of the fact that almost everyone grows up and grows old in some variation or other of a family setting, and every family setting includes someone growing up and/or growing older. There is not even a popular single term to express as one entity what is usually thought of as family (or a similar term) *and* individual development (or a similar term).

The one way in which the two areas together seem like a marriage, aside from cohabitation, is that there is often visible rivalry and jockeying for advantage and now and then an audible interest in divorce.

Underlying the differences between developmental concerns and more social concerns, if these two terms will suffice, there are two distinct social structures. Two sets of journals exist, along with differing professional organizations, different national meetings, and different sets of theoretical positions. Furthermore, the different theoretical positions are different in kind, give or take a little. One major feature of the qualitative differences in theorizing makes it most unlikely, in my opinion, that a theoretical or empirical synthesis of real power will be forthcoming in the near future.

Suppose an investigator is interested in understanding the behavior of an automobile. One way to imagine the meaning of such an interest would be in terms of the internal works of the car and the road conditions the car must face. Ultimately, if this is what "understanding" means, there would be statements about displacement, turning radius, suspension system, maximum rate of acceleration and stopping, and such environmental matters as traction conditions of the roadway, sharpness of curves, and maximum slope of inclines. It would be a very different investigation with very different outcome statements if "understanding" referred to what the driver of the car was trying to do. Is the driver trying to get to St. Louis or to New Orleans? Is the driver interested in safety or in risk-taking? Does the driver enjoy attractive scenery along the way, or would the driver want the simplest, most direct route, without regard for visual attractiveness? Answers to each of these questions would lead to a great deal of information about the behavior to be expected from the automobile, and the information would have little to do with internal works or road conditions unless they were so extreme as to thwart the driver's intentions, or unless the driver's intentions referred to these matters in some way. The driver, for instance, might refuse to drive anything but a high performance car, or might be disinclined to subject an expensive vehicle to anything but ideal roadways. Thus, one way to understand "automobile behavior" is by understanding the physical and chemical substrate of its performance. The automobile is understood as a physical product of modern science and engineering. The other way is to understand "automobile behavior" in terms of the intentions of the person driving the automobile.

Substrate is thus contrasted with *intentionality*. Confusing these two modes of understanding can be an occasion for humor, as in the old saw that the most crucial nut in an automobile is the one holding the steering wheel. Combining the two modes to form a more complete understanding seems at first glance to be the logical and simple thing to do, and so it might be if certain complications can be dealt with effectively. However, the combining to be done may be really a matter of addition, with little or no conceptual integration. That is, one would imagine a car with such and such capacities, in an environment with such and such physical characteristics, and put this together as one collection of facts. One would then imagine a driver who wants to do such and such, and who prefers such and such conditions, and then organize this information into a second group of facts. Finally, one would imagine what the particular driver at hand would do with the particular car at hand, considering both the driver's wants and the extent to which the physical facts of the situation facilitate or hinder the satisfaction of the driver's wants. Unless one has special, relevant interests, as in being a designer who wishes to build cars that will facilitate some interests and hinder others, the odds are that this last conceptual step will not be very exciting. Putting the two groups of facts together may add little to what is implied by each separately.

Within a wide range of currently true physical facts, the physical facts of a legally operable automobile are largely irrelevant to many questions about behavior that refer to the driver's intentions. Most cars will take you to a variety of different destinations, with the choice of destination entirely up to you. On the other hand, performance estimates based on physical facts of the automobile can be almost totally meaningless without quite specific assumptions about a driver's intentions. They are often put in terms of maxima and minima that an ordinary driver in an ordinary traffic situation will never test. To put it another way, these substrate implications are conditional assertions referring to what will happen if such and such driver intentions apply. As such, they are unaffected by the driver's actual intentions.

There are several generalizations that, in my opinion, go beyond this simple matter of an automobile. For one thing, substrate and intentionality views are not symmetrical to each other. One speaks of what the driver will do with the car, but not (usually) of what the car will do with the driver. Substrate facts typically relate to abilities, or to other physical facts such as attractiveness, that are like abilities in that they help to set limits on what can or cannot be done. Substrate facts define a range of possibilities within which a person with intentions can carry out choices or affect the ease or difficulty with which choices can be carried out. Finally, one can imagine a human being from a substrate orientation, but one feels awkward in imagining a machine with intentions.

To imagine an inanimate machine with intentions is almost to imagine that it is animate. By the same token, to imagine a person whose behavior is largely controlled by substrate factors is to imagine that the person is very like a machine.

It can be seen that the distinction between substrate and intentionality is another distinction that can be regarded, at least partly, as a matter of fact, and that can also be regarded largely as relating to point of view.

It is possible to regard a person totally as a machine, albeit with feelings. In fact, this is a point of view with some substantial following. The extreme machine or substrate orientation toward people may be thought more scientific than a more middling view, as if denying one of the most prominent aspects of one's naive perceptions makes one a better observer.

It can be asserted that we only feel that we make choices, whereas science knows (how?) that every choice is totally determined in advance. Thus the deterministic point of view eliminates consideration of intentions. More subtly, intentions themselves can be regarded as things, as aspects of the human mechanism not different in kind from, say, strength or visual acuity. This has its implications for clinical work. A client who has chosen to regard her/his own intentions as things feels no responsibility for them, usually as a part of a generalized passivity that does not bode well for the client's therapeutic (or other) accomplishments, unless of course one regards the passivity itself as motivated and perhaps as a brilliantly executed accomplishment.

What is substrate from one point of view may thus be intention from another. Just as it is possible to take an extreme substrate orientation, people's actions also can be regarded as almost totally a matter of intention. Almost total disregard of abilities and other physical facts can appear to be a loss of almost nothing in understanding what people do.

One way to regard psychotherapy, or at least the kind of psychotherapy to be most discussed in this collection of essays, is that it is a situation in which an absolutely determined point of view is taken on the side of intentionality. No amount of verbal denial and no explication of environmental compulsions and restraints is allowed to diminish the therapist's clear conviction that each and every outcome for a client is shaped substantially by the client's wishes. This point of view can seem absurd, as when a client is late "only" because of a flat tire or a snow storm (or both), but also it can have great power in helping a client recognize something about his or her intentions. It can turn out that the client sat inside and watched the snow storm through a window, looking all the time at the car's flat tire, until the usual (sunny-day-with-no-complications) time to leave.

Abilities, even such abilities as strength or visual acuity, can be regarded as indirect expressions of intentions, since a person can build strength by choosing appropriate diet and exercise, and can also reduce visual acuity by making appropriate choices. Physical attractiveness is a good example of something that appears at first glance to be a matter of substrate, an aspect of the organism to be dealt with in some way, but that on closer examination appears largely to reflect the organism's desired presentation of self. Turning back to the automobile, it is no novelty to observe that the car is to some extent an extension of its owner's personality. The automobile we usually drive, and hence its physical capabilities, is/are largely the product of our choices.

If a middling orientation is taken, some attributes (such as strength, visual acuity, kind of automobile driven) that change slowly over time can be thought to move back and forth between substrate and intention. Substrate facts affect subsequent intentions, which affect subsequent substrate facts, and so on. There is nothing, however, in such chains of events that actually prevents a really determined observer from regarding an entire chain as being completely a matter of substrate or almost completely a matter of intentions.

Putting together what has been said so far, human activity—let us leave automobiles behind for now—can be regarded as partly a function of intentions and partly a function of substrate facts, or it can be regarded totally as a function of substrate, or it can be regarded almost totally as a function of intentions. In their extreme forms, both points of view ignore things a naive observer might find obvious. The extreme substrate orientation cannot get a person actually to *do* much of anything without taking apparent motives themselves and turning them into things, learned on the basis of some reinforcement history or built in by instinct. The appearance of free choice is regarded as a very fancy perceptual illusion. Extreme intentionality ignores the "obvious" perception that people often want to do things they cannot do or feel compelled to do things they would rather avoid.

It may be pointless to regard a substrate view or an intentionality view as either right or wrong in the sense that if one is correct the other must be incorrect. They are, in large part, not assertions about reality but rather are stands taken about the nature of reality. As such, either point of view or both can be correct, even about the same aspect of behavior, but perhaps not at the same time.

The choice of point of view must depend at least partly on one's purposes and on how well a particular point of view is congenial to those purposes. For example, science may be well served sometimes by a substrate orientation, while clinical work often may be better served by adopting an intentionality orientation, which leads to views that seem to conflict with each other because the location of the observer is not taken into account.

However, choosing a point of view may not be solely a matter of the observer's purposes. It is possible to regard the intentionality-substrate distinction itself with some mix of intentionality and substrate. The (meta) view expressed above emphasizes the extent to which there is some choice in regarding behavior as expressing intentionality or as expressing substrate, depending on the interests—the intentions—of the observer. But perhaps we would be wise to believe that there are limits to this free choice. At the least, there may be factors inherent in a kind of subject matter—in a sense these would be meta-substrate factors—that make one orientation or the other more attractive or more plausible.

One limit may be that it is not possible to regard both points of view as correct with reference to the same aspect of behavior at the same time. At any given moment, for a given aspect of behavior, an observer will go one way or the other.

For example, obsessional behavior can be thought of as a flaw built into an organism early in life. An adult with such a flaw must either repair it or learn to live in such a way that the discomfort it brings is minimized. Alternatively, obsessional behavior can be thought of as an option that a person has selected because it seems to bring the maximum psychic gains at the smallest cost. While an observer might well hold one or the other of these views, or perhaps even both, the phenomenology of observers makes it very difficult to hold both views simultaneously. The two views lead to discriminably different accounts of the same episode of observed activity. One account of obsessionality is likely to emphasize a person's efforts in the face of an adversity, while the other is likely to emphasize the way that "adversity" is actively sought and maintained.

An account that attempts to combine the two views might emphasize conflict between a wish to avoid the symptom and a wish to enact it, but this would be only an intentionality account once removed. Enacted behavior would be seen as a compromise of sorts between two conflicting wishes, as in the traditional psychodynamic definition of symptom.

Thus, substrate and intentionality views can both be correct, but it is unlikely that they can be applied to the same behavior at the same time. Reality does change depending on where you are when you look at it. One can look at it from different points of view, and notice that all resulting perceptions are plausible—given their points of view—but it is not so easy to stand in two different places at once.

Absolute or almost absolute limits to one side, it seems clear that some aspects of reality lend themselves better to one view or the other. Substrate refers more to limits. It puts greater stress on invariance, that is, on the necessity of a particular action or on the inflexibility of some limit at a given time. Intentionality emphasizes variance or the movement back and forth of an organism within the limits that are built into it or that it has acquired. In the more extreme versions of these orientations, these distinctions tend to vanish, since by definition the extreme orientations attempt to explain almost everything from only one point of view. In the middle range, apparent invariance and flexibility seem to have something to do with the way we see the phenomena we study.

Furthermore, the rapidity with which things change may have something to do with the plausibility of one orientation or the other. A crying toddler walks around the floor with its hands up in the air. When someone picks up the child, the crying stops instantly. In such a case an observer's inclination may be to label the crying "phony," that is, the crying was not due to substrate causes (unhappiness thought to be beyond the child's immediate control), but was enacted to serve an obvious intention (getting picked up). Suppose the toddler goes on crying for a while after being picked up. In this case the observer may be more likely to regard the crying as due to such states of the organism as physical or emotional pain. Some observers might also be more likely to regard the crying as "real" or as "better" toddler behavior.

In a relatively naturalistic look at relatively normal adult human beings, most of us are struck by the pervasive appearance of intentionality in what we see. People claim to make choices and seem to do so. They even seem to do so when they claim not to. Dyads and even families sometimes strike an observer the same way: They seem to be trying to do certain things. Even if an observer is unwilling to regard a family as one animal with its own set of intentions, an observer is quite likely to be impressed with the complicated interplay of individual intentions as it shapes outcomes that may or may not appear to suit any given person's wants. One might even attempt a view that mixes a family and an individual approach, as in the suggestion that the family is sacrificing a child in some way to save itself, while no single person in the family has any such wish.

By and large, substrate factors seem more prominent in child behavior, and the younger the child the more prominent these factors seem. Children may be a much more ideal entity for one enamored of *l'homme machine* than are adults simply because so much more of what they do seems to be a function of their limited abilities. To return to the automobile analogy one last time, the efficiency of gasoline use—plausibly a substrate fact—assumes much more visibility in accounting for what cars do when the price of gasoline increases greatly. To take a more humble example, when the (substrate) shoe pinches, it gets noticed.

Thus, people are likely to speak of what adults *want* to do but of what children *can* do. Some kinds of adults are like children in this sense of attracting a substrate orientation, notably psychotics and severely retarded adults. Retarded persons, almost by definition, are understood on the basis of their limits. If there is some concern for getting the rest of us to regard retarded persons as real persons, is not this partly a matter of asserting that, in spite of more casual perceptions to the contrary, they too have feelings and wants? Psychotic persons seem severely limited in abilities, but they also may do some things "normal" people cannot. The main thing about psychotics is that they are crazy. That is, what they do makes no sense, which is to say that what they do is not readily understandable in terms of ordinary (sane) intentions. In other words, if the limits on a person's activity command our attention, or if no familiar pattern of motives makes sense of the activity, we tend to think in terms of substrate.

Studies of children may be like this even if they are of central tendencies rather than of limits. For example, average extent of social interaction might be compared at several ages instead of trying to determine the earliest age at which some form of interaction appears. These comparisons between age levels would seem to make little sense except in substrate terms. The distinction between studies of central tendency and studies of limits may be only a distinction between studying the ability of the average child and the maximum ability of any child. Studies of individual differences, say in sociability, are likely to be regarded as differences in social ability rather than as differences in what a child might choose.

Obviously, not all child development work is on abilities or even other matters of substrate. The point is that children, more than most adults, attract a substrate view. Similarly, adults, singly or together, or together with children, seem more likely to attract an intentionality view. Those conceptualizations of adults that focus on substrate seem to emphasize substrate terms that are surrogates for intentions. That is, the important terms tend to be those that explain choices whether they are expressed as intentions, as cumulations of habit strength, or simply as behavioral vectors. One way to understand studies of socialization is as a kind of interface between adult and child study that is at the same time an interface between intentionality and substrate, that is, adults may be regarded as intentional and are seen to do things that shape children who are regarded from a substrate orientation. To the extent that socialization studies are primarily concerned with outcomes for children, they may tend to express a primarily substrate orientation.

Returning to the observation that child development and family relations tend to coexist without real conceptual integration, it seems reasonable to suppose that this is related to the differences in subject matter described above, and the related differences in dominant conceptual orientation—substrate being dominant for child development and intentionality being more dominant for the study of adults and relationships that involve adults. When applied to the same activities, these two points of view are very difficult to integrate, and when applied to different aspects of activity they tend to be largely irrelevant to each other. In a study of children, motivation may be primarily important as a matter of fully involving all subjects in the experimental procedure. In a study of adult intentions, physical limits may be so taken for granted as to be quite invisible to the investigator. They may define the range of options among which subjects may choose but are not usually a matter of great concern. Furthermore, once investigations are undertaken from one point of view or the other, the investigator may be led progressively further into a consideration of phenomena for which the other point of view seems unsuitable.

Some dominance of substrate concerns among developmentalists may be related also to the way life-span development is itself developing. Concern with substrate may be leading to more emphasis on the extremes of life than with the middle portion, since getting old, like childhood, is a time in which limits pinch enough to command our attention.

By definition, development is concerned with how some things change over time. Presumably, change over time in intentions could be a focus of attention. It seems, however, that change over time has been discussed and studied more often with an emphasis on substrate. Studies of child development that detail the supposed growth of abilities over the years are an almost trivial case in point. Less trivial, in my opinion, are the stage conceptualizations of development, including at least those of Freud, Piaget, and Erickson. Wishes and fears may be used as terms in stage conceptualizations, but fundamentally each seems to speak of relative success or failure at stages in a developmental ladder, and each relative success or failure seems thought to set limits or otherwise to constrict or expand the range of possibilities at later times. Speaking as an outsider looking in, child development through adolescence sometimes seems to be an empirical data base that shows how one's range of (current) possibilities grows through the years and a conceptual base that is largely concerned with how one's (later) possibilities shrink through the years. In either case, there is a substrate emphasis on limits and possibilities.

Intentionality is the naive point of view we are most likely to adopt toward ourselves and even more toward our intimates. It is a very handy orientation when one is angry, since it supposes that a real person lives inside someone's behavioral shell, and hence that there is someone to hold responsible and to blame. A kind of substrate view is also handy in that we regularly diagnose our spouses and enemies, as in, "You are just *sick.*" This however is a pretty ambiguous use of substrate, since the object of the diagnosis may be held responsible for being "sick" and thought able to change. Alternatively, the accusation that a person's behavior comes from a faulty substrate is almost a death wish, since it suggests that inside the external shell of behavior there is not a real person calling the shots but only an illness. People are not flattered by being regarded as machines. They are diminished phenomenologically. Yet they may welcome this diminishment.

It is a regular and mundane occurrence in clinical work that a person (or couple, or family) wants a prescription, be it chemical or behavioral. *L'homme* (or *femme*) *machine* cannot be blamed for her/his/its actions and their consequences and cannot be held responsible for the difficult business of changing. If the "doctor" prescribes something, the doctor has become the machine operator to some extent and to that extent the "patient" can relax. In my opinion, the patient's life becomes slightly less (or fails to become more) at the same time as it becomes easier. This is hypnosis in a small way: The joint pretense that one's behavior is the work of a real (intentional) person but that the intentional person is the hypnotist and not oneself the subject.

Although intentionality seems to be the view that is most often taken naively about ourselves, and perhaps about most adults, it is readily regarded as merely one mythological entity, albeit one that is more interesting than the evanescent behavior it is invoked to "explain." As such, there is no particular reason to limit intentionality-oriented views to individual persons. If a person need not be regarded as a machine, then perhaps one need not regard a couple or a family as a machine either. Here may be a situation in which the raw observed activity calls out more for a substrate orientation than for intentionality but in which intentionality might be an orientation that makes much sense out of apparent chaos. Just because no one of us can actually *be* a couple or larger group, can we not imagine that such groups may be like us in terms of intentionality? If we can, is it possible that the exercise, now that we have thought about systems for some years, might be a useful one? Without pursuing these questions further for now, it might be mentioned that computer users sometimes speak of even an inanimate program (not its programmer) as having expectations and wants and seem to be bothered very little by the animism involved.

For some reason there appears to be a status difference between intentionality and a substrate orientation. Perhaps it has to do with the scientific interest in exactitude and predictability. Highly deterministic phenomena are, perhaps by definition, more predictable than what appears to be "free" choice and hence may be thought to be more scientific. There is a slight difficulty here in that conceptualizing something in terms of its predictability does not actually make it more predictable, so it is possible that a substrate orientation may be preferred occasionally more for its scientific style than for its aid in accomplishment. Also, the phenomena most commonly described in terms of abilities, limits, and other substrate characteristics of persons may in fact be more predictable than the more variable phenomena that are most usually thought of as motivational. Either way, it does seem that the substrate point of view has higher status in academic circles (and sometimes in clinical ones), leading to further complications if one wishes a happy cohabitation of the two stances.

The easy editorial here is that happy cohabitation—bureaucratically, personally, or professionally—may be a matter of live and let live with a tolerant attitude toward occasional (acknowledged) borrowing. It is difficult to see why one conceptual or epistemological stance ought to have more status than another, or why choosing to study limits ought to be more prestigious than studying phenomena that seem less predictable. It seems likely, also, that conceptual integration is unlikely or is likely to be intellectually trivial. Here I should acknowledge that I am not so sure this last point is correct. In fact, it would be very nice to be shown wrong. However, an integration would need to take into account the substrate-intentionality distinction, or some similar distinction, and pay attention to the possibility of inconsistencies among points of view. Some things cannot be reconciled with each other, even in science, even while each—understood from its own point of view—might in some way be correct or at least plausible.

The real steam behind this essay—its latent intentionality, so to speak—is not, however, the desire to urge mutual toleration among colleagues or even to note that some concepts cannot be well integrated. It has more to do with the feeling that this distinction between points of view has some general importance in our work and even in our lives, partly because it may be closely related to our ideas about real persons as opposed to things. As the objects of our study seem more like complete human beings, intentionality becomes relatively more attractive, and as they seem limited or infirm from being old or very young, retarded, or crazy, or as we put more distance between them and us, a substrate view seems to feel better to us, the observers.

Perhaps it is true that a thoroughgoing substrate orientation is really the way to go for much of social science. If so, it is to be expected that social scientists will continue to be accused of taking a diminished view of what it is to be human, because the accusation will be true. It will not be the clinicians but the scientists who more properly deserve to be called "shrinks."

Intentionality, in short, may have something more to be said for it than it usually receives, even in consideration of relatively normal adults. It deserves serious consideration in understanding the activity of individual humans, and people in groups. Some of us might even be willing to flirt with intentionality as one way to approach humanlike or human-created inanimate systems. It is even possible that intentions rather than "activity" might be a legitimate *object* of inquiry.

In effect, this is speaking up in part for a point of view that is less concerned with limits and limitlike aspects of the people we study, in the context of essays that as a whole urge more attention to our limits as observers. To restate one theme of this entire essay collection, there may be more to learn about our subject matter, and more limitations in our ability to acquire this learning, than we might like to believe.

There are thus two points here. One is the old and humdrum point that substrate-oriented science must expect to pay a social price for its point of view. The second point is the slightly less careworn view that substrate is not necessarily always the way to go even if one is solely interested in science.

There is also a third point, which is that when we regard ourselves as substrate, we feel and perhaps are diminished. As clinicians, we also diminish our clients in our minds, that is, we see them more as cases and less as whole people, when we look at them and see mostly substrate. Even if an extreme substrate orientation *is* the way to go for basic science, we might want to think a bit about its implications if we adopt it in our personal lives or as clinicians. If an extreme substrate orientation is indeed the way to go for science, and if some of us choose not to pay the price for adopting it in our personal lives or clinical work, does that mean that there are limits *in principle* to the usefulness of (substrate-oriented) science to (intentionality-oriented) clinical work?

6

WANTING VERSUS CARING

Looking back through Western civilization, there is a basic distinction between two kinds of feelings that are both referred to as love and a corresponding distinction between two ways of construing feelings. *Theories of Attraction and Love* (Murstein, 1971) included five essays on the general subject of attraction and one that focused explicitly on the idea of love. In that one essay, Walster introduced her theory of passionate love. She made some editorial comments in passing on the ambiguously respectable nature of studying such a topic. She seemed to suggest that, at least until recently, those who wanted to study love would be courting snickers from their colleagues and would not be welcomed by granting agencies. Love, it seems, has been something of an embarrassment.

Even the Walster essay spoke not so much of love as of the passion that may sometimes accompany it. She apparently sought to make love respectable by casting it in scientifically respectable terms.

Passionate love, she said, is a "distinct emotional state which a person might experience if (1) he is physiologically aroused, and (2) he concludes that love is the appropriate label for his aroused feelings." There is a respectable concreteness and touch of cynicism here, and the idea of love seems just a little trivialized. True, passionate love must include passion of some kind, and perhaps people sometimes do refer to emotional upheavals as love simply for want of a better label. Somehow, there is still something missing. Love itself seems somehow to have been left out.

Social scientists could not have shied away from love simply because they avoid topics about which they have personal feelings. Too many studies of marriage satisfaction have been carried out for that idea to be plausible. The problem could not have been simply that love is too complex to conceptualize clearly. The work of Rubin (1970) or of Lee

(1976) shows how readily that problem can be circumvented although at a price like that paid by Walster.

On the face of it, love is very difficult to ignore in dealing with close interpersonal relationships. It is virtually impossible to talk to people about their marriages without hearing about love or its absence. Almost certainly, at some time in our lives each of us has said, "I love you," and—and this is the important point—we have believed that we were telling the truth. So here is a phenomenon that is reported by almost everyone, believed in at some level by each of us, and which as a consequence intrudes itself into studies of close relationships at every turn.

Perhaps the odd way love has been dealt with will become a little more understandable as we get into definitional matters and the basic distinction between two points of view toward love. This distinction will be used in arguing that difficulties in dealing with love come in part from cultural history, from a confusion between kinds of feelings and ways of construing feelings, from nonscientific and control-oriented precursors of modern behaviorism, and perhaps even from the "nothing but" idolatrous world view of science in general. Then there will be a more or less metaphoric discussion of communes, and some comments on passionate love (drawing somewhat on the twelfth-century views of Andreus the Chaplain, 1959).

At the end it will be suggested that considering love can indeed lead one right out of science. Alternatively, it can suggest a choice in the way one views science. Perhaps the discerning reader will see that this lengthy discussion of love is really an extended editorial on social science. Or is it that this book is really an extended editorial about love?

The Basic Distinction

Personally, I love steak. In my more vegetarian moods, I feel guilty about loving steak, because it seems to me that my attitude involves a certain amount of unkindness to cows. Is this just a special case of, "You always hurt the one you love," or am I somehow using language in a peculiar way? We might say too that cats love mice. Too bad for the mice. Would we therefore mean something different by the word love if we said, "John loves Mary"? It seems more or less obvious that John's love for Mary might or might not mean the same thing as my love for steak. It depends. What about the love a human being might feel for

God? Well, if you mean God in a Platonist sense, the answer might very well be that a person loves God in the same way I love steak or that cats love mice; but in the Christian tradition the answer is not as clear. What about God's love for people? Well, in the Christian tradition God's love for people is very much not the kind of thing I feel for steak, except in a very roundabout way, and in the Platonist tradition the question is absurd. What, crudely speaking, passes for God in that tradition—that is, the ultimate good—loves nothing.

There are two basically different but easily confused kinds of definitions for loving or liking. These two kinds of definitions have to do, respectively, with *taking* and with *giving*. If we are to be more concerned with feelings than with actions, we might put them in terms of *wanting* and *caring*. When I say that I love steak, I am using the word love in a very conventional and everyday way, referring to my interest in the pleasure and satisfaction I receive from steak. Feelings of unselfish concern for the steak itself are nil, although the touch of guilt I feel suggests possibly a twinge of concern for the cow it came from.

Taking some liberties with terminology, in trying to convey what is presently meant rather than to be historically precise, we can say that the wanting orientation is analogous to the idea of *eros* (Gould, 1963). That is, eros is the striving after or the attraction to that which will bring one the most happiness. That which is most good is by definition that which will bring one the most happiness; therefore, one loves or is attracted to the good. At the most abstract level there is the ultimate good toward which persons are ultimately attracted if they are sufficiently enlightened. If ultimate good is to be personified, it is clearly without love (eros), since there is nothing from which it can gain benefit.

Agape is something else again. Agape is almost by definition not deserved, that is, it has nothing to do with what the lover gets out of it. As Singer (1966) put it, there is a bestowal of love as a gift. Thus, the Christian God loves us all even though we are sinners and unworthy. The poor, the humble, and our enemies are to be loved, not because it brings us profit, but because it is good to bestow love.

Caritas is almost but not quite a kind of blend of eros and agape, in that we cherish and freely bestow caring, and yet we receive and enjoy happiness and satisfaction.

It would be easy to regard taking as the same thing as giving but in the opposite direction. Then, eros and agape could be thought of as quite symmetrical. Except that the object to be benefited by eros is the self, and the object to be benefited by agape is another, they would be identical. In the present essay, however, this usage is not quite what is intended. The distinction is important in considering caritas, since caritas is thought of as a caring and giving attitude whether directed toward oneself or toward oneself and another.

There are three distinctions between giving to oneself and taking. First, there is a distinction between accepting oneself as one is, wanting and all, rather than insisting that one straighten up and acquire X, Y, and Z. Eros consists more of demand than acceptance. Second, the affective aspect of caring, the warmth and satisfaction, seems different from the affect associated with acquisition. Third, the relationship between the self and others is different. The difference is between caring for oneself *and* others, and wanting things for oneself *versus* others getting them. There is a difference between generosity that includes the self and selfishness. Hence caritas, while seeming more like eros than does agape, is thought of here as being distinct from eros.

Turning back to tradition, even the distinction between eros and agape is not entirely clear-cut. The point of view associated with each can be used to encompass all love. Even the Christian God is not being entirely generous, since ultimately God is loving God. Agape travels from God to humanity, and something more like eros travels from humanity back to God. Also, Plato did not characterize eros as base selfishness. In the long run, that which is most beautiful is most good and is best for oneself. It is simply a mistake to be attracted to satisfactions that are superficial, short-sighted, or that are more a matter of self-protection than of reaching for the stars.

Still, these are different views of love. To use either one in characterizing all love is to emphasize some aspects of feeling and to minimize others. The aspects emphasized by these two points of view correspond to a fairly clear difference between feelings that are directed toward taking, such as eros, and feelings that are directed toward giving, such as agape or caritas.

Social scientists have a problem, to which we shall return, in even trying to conceptualize a motivation the satisfaction of which does not bring one satisfaction. Perhaps it should be pointed out that agape can be viewed as an inclination to do something where the benefit implicitly in mind is fairly indirect or ultimate. One casts bread upon the waters, as it were, trusting that eventually and indirectly one will benefit.

Another way to view giving to others is to suggest that the giver, or lover, feels or does things for another person but experiences them as if they were done for oneself. Freud (1962) distinguished between narcissistic love, in which the loved object is experienced to some extent as an aspect of oneself, and love of the anaclitic type, in which love depends on what one receives from the loved object.

Distinctions similar to those between eros and caritas, if not agape, can be found in the sphere of economic and political views. In exaggerated and simplified form, the rightist idea has been traditionally that if each pursues her or his interests, maximum good will result for all. The corresponding simplification of the traditional leftist view is that if each acts for the good of all, the result will be the maximum good, on the average, for each.

Finally, no historical overview of ideas concerning love, however synoptic, can ignore the emergence of romantic or courtly love. Courtly love might be seen in part as an aspect of the general cultural turmoil in the centuries following Christianity's greatest failure: The world failed to come to an end, as predicted, in A.D. 1000. Some of the mysticism associated with religion now became associated with human relationships. The structural model of relationships was based on the myth of Tristan und Isolde (de Rougemont, 1956). One person strove mightily to overcome almost insurmountable obstacles in order to acquire, to win, another. Acquiring is a Platonist, eros-oriented idea, hence romantic or courtly love, at its inception, can be thought of as Platonist love overlaid with a certain patina of Christian culture. In other words, courtly love is one kind of mystified Platonism.

Note one last time the caveat that various theological and political terms used here are being employed in a metaphorical rather than a strictly literal sense in order to suggest some shared cultural heritage for distinctions to be made in religion, politics, and personal affectional relationships. There is thus some historical rationale and some cultural support for the idea that there are two conceptually distinct aspects of relationships among people. In intimate interpersonal situations both aspects may be referred to as love. Also, it is important to be aware that the distinction being discussed does not just refer to two aspects of relationships among people but also to two ways of thinking about relationships among people. The Platonist view has acquired such a hold over contemporary social science, as mentioned earlier, that it is difficult even to conceptualize a giving orientation without reformulating it as a disguised form of taking.

Platonist Bias

The single most prominent force in contemporary social science is still reductionist behaviorism with a determinedly Platonist bias. Two paths can be taken in suggesting that such a view is not an essential one—that it is not necessitated by the observable facts (and hence that it is a choice). One path is by way of pointing to a nonscientific or cultural antecedent for the behaviorist viewpoint. It could be said that behaviorism has arisen, in part, for historical rather than for scientific reasons. The other path is to at least allude to the possibility that nonbehaviorist, non-Platonist, in short, nonhedonist formulations are not obvious nonsense. Perhaps it can be suggested, although not proven, that the Platonist view is not absolutely, logically required.

Considering the first of these two paths, a very general critique is possible along the lines taken by Theodore Roszak (1972), whose thoughts are also cited elsewhere in these pages. Roszak argues that for historical and cultural reasons, science in general—and social science in particular—is bound basically and at its center to a reductionist, "nothing but" single-vision value system, in which events are necessarily stripped of nonscientific meaning. We might add that the meaning which is stripped off is precisely the kind of meaning that informs the idea of love. For present purposes, however, it should be satisfactory to take a more narrow position, to say that even within a scientific framework, a reductionist ("nothing but") view of intimate relationships has at least some roots elsewhere than in the observable facts. The behaviorist orientation, for example, has at least some background in the history of that form of magical interpersonal control usually known as hypnosis (once known as animal magnetism).

Animal magnetism was an expression originally meant literally to the extent that physical magnets were sometimes employed. Franz Anton Mesmer himself used idiosyncratic clothing, exotic hardware, and an elaborated conceptual framework that encompassed nothing less than the universe. Much later Jean Martin Charcot at the Salpêtrière, who was much more respectable than was Mesmer, nonetheless used fairly exotic conceptual formulations and a wide variety of elaborated effects that were thought to result from hypnosis.

Bernheim and Liebault, at Nancy, formulated their own view of hypnotic phenomena and suggested that the phenomena were much simpler and less exotic than was believed by the people at the Salpêtrière. A model of the nervous system was suggested in which stimuli came into a lower nervous center, went up to a higher nervous center where they were processed in some way, and then returned to the lower nervous center and generated responses. Hypnosis worked "simply" by suggestion and short circuited the usual nervous system process. Stimuli came into the lower nervous center and immediately exited again as responses in a so-called psychomoter reaction.

In other words, there was on one hand a school of thought in which hypnosis was viewed as a complicated and obscure set of phenomena, with many diverse aspects understandable by and indeed only demonstrable by the elite experts at the Salpêtrière. The other school of thought emphasized a "nothing but" attitude, fairly simple formal abstractions, and the idea of explaining widely diverse consequences with a simple conceptual building block, namely suggestion.

Freud seems to have had a foot in both camps, but was perhaps more influenced by the Salpêtrière. Certainly the flavor of his formulations, and even more so those of some of the people around him, retained the note of ineffable complexity that characterized the Salpêtrière point of view and that might be said to have originated with Mesmer. For present purposes, we might note particularly the psychoanalytic emphasis on the possibility of people behaving in ways that do not seem immediately to be in their own self-interest and that are gratifying in subtle or indirect ways.

Another direction of the Salpêtrière influence was in the trait psychology that imagines that abstractions based on questionnaires or other measures somehow represent real entities inside people's heads. Binet was at the Salpêtrière and involved in the Salpêtrière school of thought regarding hypnosis.

On the other hand, the Nancy school of Bernheim and Liebault, with some possible ties to Braid, is connected to at least two other subsequent developments. One is the neo-Nancy school of Emile Coué, the man who urged people to improve themselves by daily repeating, "Every day in every way I am getting better and better." Coué's intellectual heirs include those who would give us simple formulas—such as positive thinking, which, if followed, will lead us to win friends, influence people, and do other desirable things.

The views of the Nancy school also found their way into the mind of the prestigious American psychologist, Clark Hull. Hull's ambitious work (1933) on hypnosis appeared to be largely an engine for demonstrating and reiterating the Nancy views. He concluded that hypnosis was nothing but a matter of suggestion. In a formulation directly derivative from the Nancy view of nervous system operation and psychomotor responses, Hull formulated the idea of a so-called pure stimulus act, which was a response having no other function than to generate stimulation for another response.

Thus, the "nothing but" school of thought concerning hypnosis was one of the intellectual parents (along with Pavlov and Thorndike) of the stimulus-response, learning theory, behaviorist, reinforcement wing of American social science. In its recent incarnation under the dominant influence of B. F. Skinner, this tradition emphasizes that much or all behavior is nothing but the outcome of reinforcement history—that is, that the most complex phenomena are explainable on the basis of a simple conceptual building block. The same orientation is also tied in, of course, with the law of effect, American pragmatism, and the capitalist-entrepreneurial—that is, Platonist—emphasis on the extent to which people do things only when they get something out of it directly and right away.

In short, it is plausible that historical antecedants and cultural setting, and not just scientific necessity, have influenced the currently dominant theoretical biases. If John loves Mary, the question must be what are the immediate and direct payoffs to John from Mary. The "nothing but" tradition must be prone to trivializing relationships, to a concern with control, and to an eros orientation. Furthermore, the principal historical rival to Platonism is only part way across the spectrum from eros to caritas, which is to say that it is one version of mystified Platonism, although different from a courtly view.

The reference here is to psychoanalytic thought, which is hardly free from a Platonist bias. Also influenced by the Mesmerist tradition, it emphasizes the complications to be found in phenomena. Psychoanalytic formulations assert that a person's interpersonal relationships have to do with what he or she gets out of them but hedge this assertion with so many qualifications and subtleties that a caritas formulation becomes somewhat more conceptually tractable.

Some time ago a much touted third force began in American psychology. This third force, the humanist movement, seemed to eschew both the intellectual complications of psychoanalytic theorizing and the rudeness of reinforcement theory and may have had its primary roots elsewhere, as in the less theologically elaborated subcultures of Christianity. Perhaps, at its most crass, it is also related to the neo-Nancy school of Coué. The humanist movement as a whole has seemed less troubled by the intellectual complications of conceptualizing altruism and more oriented toward viewing human relationships in terms of the kind of phenomena referred to here as caritas. Platonist bias is, however, to be found here and there in what used to be called the encounter group movement, in some aspects of Gestalt therapy, and elsewhere, encompassing even generous acts under the general rubric of doing things that make oneself feel good. Albert Ellis, the Ayn Rand of humanistic psychology, has been a particularly curious example, devoting his life to making other people happier by insisting that realistic selfishness is the only sensible worldview.

Thus there are roughly three distinguishable intellectual traditions, variously susceptible to the Platonist viewpoint. The "nothing but" orientation, still mostly dominant in academic psychology, and in part traceable back to a particular kind of concern with hypnotism (and hence control), is an orientation that seems almost to require a Platonist construction. The intellectual complications of psychoanalysis, and the emphasis on gut feelings of some humanists, are more hospitable to an acknowledgement of caring, but they too are not free of Platonism.

The full range of love phenomena, including both eros and caritas, just does not fit well into any of the major social science traditions. That may be one reason it has been studied relatively little. At the least it would be no anomaly for a proposal to study love from a caritas orientation to be judged unscientific by a partisan of pragmatic, entrepreneurial, "nothing but," control-oriented social science.

Hence, it is argued that tradition has made caritas, much less agape, difficult even to conceptualize. Altruism has been shirked for reasons that are as much cultural as scientifically required. Possibly too, the Platonist viewpoint has such a strong grip on contemporary social science not so much because of its correctness as because of its usefulness. It is a handy position to have if one is interested in controlling others' behavior or in getting things from them (which is to say it is an attractive point of view for those who are themselves involved in wanting, and who have an interest in control). The Platonist view has become so pervasive that it does not seem to require proof. It has acquired a certain obviousness to the extent that the very idea of unselfish sharing seems absurd on the face of it.

There is also a second path that can be taken in arguing that altruism is imaginable, that it is conceptually feasible.

One can turn to a real or hypothetical bit of observed activity and at least allude to the possibility that a Platonist interpretation is not required by the facts. The Platonist viewpoint cannot actually be proven wrong, any more than it can be proven right (as a total explanation for all observed events), since in part it is a stand taken rather than a matter of fact.

Suppose, however, we consider a hypothetical series of events. One person does something nice for another person, and feels good about it. Subsequently, the same person does something nice for another person and again feels good about it. And so on. One point of view is indeed that the behavior in question is only apparently altruistic. People really do nice things for the selfish reason that it makes them feel good. But there is a second point of view that is equally consistent with the facts. A partisan of the caritas view might be likely to explain the feeling good by the altruistic conduct. That is, the explanation of the person's feeling good is that it usually feels good to do something nice, and this person has done something nice.

To be sure, the second mode of explanation has not particularly explained the generous behavior. But by the same token, the first mode of explanation has not explained the feeling good. In general, reinforcement theory cannot explain reinforcements except in terms of other reinforcements. It must go beyond its own scope as in the "explanation" that certain reinforcements are simply and biologically *there*.

The point I am trying to get across is that one can use the associated feelings to explain altruism or one can use altruism to explain the associated feelings. We will pass over the fact that these are both reductionist explanations and that from a third point of view the acts and the feelings form part of a system that cannot reasonably be disentangled into cause and effect.

The question of how there got to be a link between altruism and feeling good is of no consequence. Whether the link exists because of human genetics or because a child was patted on the head at appropriate times, a later (reductionist) observer will still have the option of using feelings to explain altruism or altruism to explain feelings. If the observer is enamored of a "nothing but" view, the explained phenomenon will be said to be nothing but the explaining phenomenon. Logically speaking, however, either feelings or altruistic actions can take either role, that is, either explained or explaining.

Perhaps there is some basis for deciding that in fact there is no such link between altruism and feeling good. Then the choice remains but in a negative way. An observer who is trying to explain (or explain away) altruism will have to look elsewhere for an explanation and will no doubt find one. The more hypothetical but equally possible observer who is trying to explain (or explain away) feeling good will also have to look elsewhere.

"Explain" and "explain away" are not exactly identical expressions. Explaining altruistic conduct by noting that it is regularly followed by feeling good is not quite the same as getting rid of it, any more than the feeling good is actually gotten rid of by using altruistic conduct to explain it. "Explain" gets turned into "explain away" when the explanation is regarded as more fundamental and more important than that which is explained. This is a matter of attitude and value judgment, not of fact.

One formal difference between the two suggested modes of explanation is that in one mode an earlier event (altruism) is being used to explain a later one (feelings), whereas in the other mode a later event is being used to explain an earlier one. In contemporary jargon it should be noted that which comes first, in a series of events such as those described earlier, is really a matter of punctuation. Most if not all altruistic acts are preceded and also followed by the feelings described and most if not all instances of good feeling are both preceded and followed by altruistic acts.

One empirical difference is that *all* altruism is popularly thought to be explained in terms of subsequent feelings, whereas I know of no one who has argued recently that all feeling good is explainable in terms of preceding altruism. In passing, note that this last alternative might be an entertaining exercise. For starters, note that expressions of comfortable and pleasant feelings tend to be bald assertions of personal worth, for example, I feel *good,* or I feel *nice.* It might be noted too that it is not the caritas but the Platonist tradition that, in its original form in the writings of Plato, comes closest to arguing for this conclusion.

The Marriage Syndrome

Turning back to a consideration of human relationships, what if any are the helpful implications of viewing love as two conceptual entities, wanting (eros) or caring (caritas)? For one thing, certain apparent paradoxes might become a little less puzzling. The idea of devouring not only the steak but also the people that one loves is not so strange if it is understood that love in such situations is more wanting than caring. The person who claims to be consumed with love for another person until, and only until, that other person is felt to have been acquired, can be assumed to have been involved with eros rather than caritas.

Conventional marriage seems often to include variations on a pattern sometimes referred to as the marriage syndrome (Ryder, Kafka, & Olson, 1971). In this pattern, one spouse, let us say the wife, works hard to extract more love from the other spouse, the husband. The wife may engage in unpleasant, demanding activities to spark some kind of life and attention from her husband. The husband, on the other hand, may want primarily to be left alone. At least that is what the husband and wife may report.

For present purposes, an individually oriented view of this situation will be taken, and the spouses' reports will be taken seriously. The husband, by his report, may attempt to turn off his wife's excited and demanding behavior, dealing with the excitement by being more calm and reasonable than ever, and dealing with the demands by attempting to meet them in some minimal way. The husband's attempts to calm his wife by being more calm himself are likely doomed to failure, since the wife is looking for more affect from him rather than less. There can be an explosive cycle of increasingly excited activity on the part of one spouse and the increasing appearance of calm and reasonableness on the part of the other.

Both spouses must be or become quite angry in this situation, and we cannot assume the husband (in this particular example) to be a complete fool. Hence it is probable that at some level of awareness the husband recognizes that his actions are not calming but provocative and is gratified by that fact. Yet even while he is angry, he may be making conscious efforts to yield to the wife's demands for love and attention, to placate her and/or to undermine the appearance of justice in her complaints. He may, for example, be consciously planning to get her in a good enough mental condition that he feels safe in leaving her.

The husband is then surprised and distressed, omitting less conscious feelings, to find that the wife is not placated at all. She is likely to say that the husband is not being really attentive and concerned with her but is only acting that way because she has demanded it.

Except for whatever comfort the husband may get from this additional evidence that his wife is unreasonable, the husband may now feel himself to be trapped. He feels now that there is absolutely no way for him to win. Indeed, both spouses may now feel thoroughly trapped. How can she express what she wants without expressing it, and how can he respond to her wishes without doing so in response to her wishes?

In this extreme example, both spouses are involved in what has been referred to as eros. Any giving between them, particularly on the part of the husband, is for immediate self-interest, and is perceived as such. Also, protests of intense love, particularly on the part of the wife, often can be seen as expressions of how much one needs or wants the other person and his attentions. The chief intrusion of caritas is in the content of the demands for attention, as the wife is saying in the most clear way possible that caritas is what she wants, and not eros. She is saying that in order to satisfy her demands the husband must do attentive things for some other reason than to satisfy her demands.

The wife in this example will recognize the kind of attentiveness she wants by certain distinguishing characteristics. (1) Caritas attention will be forthcoming when it would be easy for the husband not to provide it, and (2) caritas attention will not turn off if she fails to reward it more or less immediately. I do believe that people may fail to trust caring that is real but that in one way or another they will not trust caring that is false, even if it is carefully arranged to seem real. There will always be subtle cues. Let us, however, keep this example simple and keep to the two features listed above. The second of these two requires a kind of long-term trust on the part of the husband—as in the idea of bread cast upon the waters. The first distinguishing feature requires not only that the husband is interested enough so that his interest is apparent when it is not being mandated but also that there *be* times when his attention is not being mandated. There must be periods of time in which the wife is willing to put herself so at risk that the husband is clearly able to deny her what she wants at little cost to him.

In real life, things are more complex. There is the interplay of unconscious fears and wishes. There is the consideration of system aspects of the interaction, perhaps involving many other people. There is the larger social scene and how it structures and coerces relationships between the sexes. Still, a consideration of love as eros and caritas seems to add a bit of information about a situation that in one form or another is very common. It even provides some basis for expectations about subsequent events, depending on the willingness of either or both partners to give and to take risks beyond those that may already have been taken.

Communes

Suppose we were to set out in a serious and goal-directed way to organize a social setting that would maximize caritas. Could we design, say, a commune of some sort that could become a visible and attractive exemplar of a caritas-oriented group? Looking at the real communes that were popular a decade or so ago, it appears that some but not all actually made such an attempt. There was a large variety of different kinds of groups, with different intentions and structures, or the absence thereof, so our task would not be to imitate an ideal case that once existed. It would be to imagine one that is ideal only in terms of the central intention to make caritas more probable, and the secondary intention of confronting society at large with a visible and attractive caritas-oriented alternative.

Given that this hypothetical group has a lifestyle or creed to advance, and some interest in evangelism, it can be assumed that among the issues to be faced are those of power structure and those of boundary conditions.

Power structure. Issues here have to do with extent of control. At one extreme a group may have a strict status hierarchy, an informal but effective power structure, or some other arrangement that effectively sanctions valued and essential activities. In extreme versions, everybody may be responsible *for* specific tasks and *to* a specific person or the group as a whole. Sometimes there have been attempts to automate control, to render the exercise of authority invisible and painless, by attaching rewards in an impersonal way to particular tasks. At the other extreme there have been groups where the explicit ideal is that each person does what seems pleasing with the proviso that it is also nice for people to please each other. A group intending to be apart from conventional society, and to avoid obligations and sanctions, might be regarded as involved in anarchy of the Left, or perhaps collectivist libertarianism. It might have an ideology stressing a blend of individual freedom and sharing.

If one is attracted by this so-called anarchy of the Left, one must come to terms with the possibility that the most attractive settings may also be the most evanescent. When everyone does what seems pleasing, there is the risk that no one will choose to do some necessary task. If no one chooses to do work related to sanitation there may be a serious risk of disease. Disease may also be a problem if too many people do not choose to avoid activities with risk attached. If there is a great deal of sexual activity among group members, disease can spread rapidly through the group and be difficult to eradicate. Also, a group based on freedom and sharing is ripe pickings for exploiters. It may take only a few people who are less interested in a combination of freedom and sharing than in a combination of freedom and taking to demoralize, change, and perhaps even end such a group.

Boundary conditions. Some groups, in effect, have been surrounded by high walls. New members have been accepted only after careful screening and perhaps even an apprenticeship. One of the qualifications for membership might have been that an individual seemed likely to be loyal and steadfast. Easy movement into or out of the group was discouraged.

At the other boundary extreme, some groups have had it as a basic tenet that anyone could walk in off the street and be, because of presence alone, a group member and as entitled as anyone else to available resources.

The Haight Ashbury neighborhood of San Francisco, in its heyday in the 1960s, might have been an illustration of such a group in an extended way. In its best days, real or only romanticized in memory, one could wander into the Haight (and into analogous neighborhoods in many other cities) and be immediately pretty much at home. One might be spoken to not as a stranger but as a comrade. One might be given dope, food, and perhaps a place to sleep. And one could as easily walk out of the Haight without causing more than a ripple in its social life.

The Haight was, or was alleged to be, a communelike neighborhood in that there was a community with a shared ethic, in this case an ethic of what has been referred to here as the anarchy of the Left. It was dramatically synthesizing in that it was a distinct neighborhood yet bound by shared values and by hundreds and perhaps thousands of migrating people with Washington Square, Dupont Circle, Jackson Square, and other foci around the country. These symbolized not only particular communities, but also a united people or folk who would lead the United States as a whole into an exciting revolution.

Haight Ashbury may be useful not only as a metaphor for a commune without walls, but also for one without well-defined rules or power structure, and one that illustrates the evanescence of such groups. The Haight changed from a relatively gentle and loving community to one less gentle and less loving, and in short order. One became less likely to offer a stranger free marijuana and more likely to ask a stranger for money, or indeed to rob the stranger. The various problems of not having rules and defined tasks are complicated by having open boundaries. In the first place, users, persons who come to take and not to give, cannot be avoided. In the second place, with no insulation from the outside world, particularly the insulation of secrecy, there is little protection from those who would attack the group and/or compel it to change. Sometimes attacks have been by the police, and with contrary results. Police activity may drive out or change gentle and nonviolent people, and have less success with those who are tough enough to defy them. Thus, police activities may sometimes have the effect of rendering their client groups and neighborhoods more tough and dangerous and, of course, more in need of police activity. Along the way, caritas is driven out.

Alternatively, groups that metaphorically have walls around them and that live protected from the unpleasantness of outside life might survive intact much longer. But by their insulation these groups may be enacting the group version of what Philip Slater (1963) once attributed to dyadic intimacy: They are dropping out, no longer contributing to or being a part of society at large. It is not that they are dropping out of conventional society but out of whatever culture is made up of those who mostly think as they do. By dropping out, say, from the cultural Left, they may be advancing personal goals but also fragmenting a social movement and destroying a chance to change the country in any fundamental way. Since groups that follow this path may no longer be a serious threat to conventional society, they might be increasingly acceptable to governmental authorities. To paraphrase only somewhat facetiously what someone once said about marijuana, perhaps some kinds of groups would be in grave danger of being legalized—that is, of being swallowed up by the present social and economic system without causing more than a ripple of change.

COMMUNITY VERSUS EXPLOITATION

The distinction between community and exploitation, as used here, is only one more expression in a particular social context of the caritas-eros distinction. A caritas or community orientation is consistent with what we have been referring to as anarchy of the Left, whereas an eros or exploitative orientation is consistent with what might be called anarchy of the Right. Another way to put the distinction in this context is between freedom with sharing and freedom with taking. The concept of quid pro quo might be useful here. In the rightist, or eros orientation, one pays as little as possible for what one receives and only provides quid pro quo if compelled to do so, as when one is dealing with another person of the same orientation. With an orientation more toward caritas, one gives, and also receives, with less thought to quid pro quo, since the very idea of quid pro quo is inconsistent with a concern for general welfare, and with a general downgrading of possessiveness.

In moving from a consideration of individuals to a consideration of groups of people, the question of how real or important caritas is is found again with particular force. Is it not naive to expect people in large numbers to really care about each other? Advocates of one position can point to instances where individuals and groups have behaved in a caring way, whereas those on the other side can usually point to the worm in each apple, and to the ease with which frustrated openness turns harsh. The hard-headed view of a giving orientation is of course that if it is not a fraud, it is certainly soft-headed. Anyone who is consistently sharing without requiring compensation is clearly not acting in his or her own self-interest. A counterargument might be that the allegedly soft-headed view is the only possible rational one. If people and groups in our society do not manage some degree of trust, and to some extent act for each other rather than just for themselves, then contemporary society will continue on a downward spiral to chaos and disaster. After all, the view that people are only decent to each other out of immediate necessity flies in the face of everyday reality. Is it not obvious that real societies are primarily held together by something akin to caritas and that those who think themselves to be hard-headed realists deceive themselves by believing otherwise?

For present purposes, the problem is that where attempts have been made to maximize sharing, usually with minimal authority structure and boundary restrictions, the results have been doubtful. Groups based solely on sharing do not seem to be very durable, and mutual trust seems generally to be a dwindling commodity. Furthermore, actions taken to raise the general level of sharing may have the opposite effect to the one apparently intended.

Imagine for the moment that you belong to a volunteer group of some sort in which each of a set of persons donates some amount of time and energy toward a common cause. Imagine further that you feel the other group members should donate more time and energy than they do. In order to encourage them to participate more, you go out of your way to set a good example and devote your every spare moment to the work of the group. The probable result is obvious. Rather than causing others to emulate you, you are likely to find that others come to depend on you to get things done. They may feel not more but less of an obligation to help out, since they know you are available to do what they fail to do. Your action does not increase but rather reduces the general level of sharing, and you are likely to regret it.

The general point is simple but disheartening. Society would probably be better off if people were more sharing, but individual efforts to achieve this result can backfire. There is this paradox about sharing: An isolated individual increasing her or his level of sharing can lead to a distinct reduction in sharing orientation on her or his own part and on that of other people. Consider the unpleasant pattern sometimes occurring in conventional marriage, which we have been referring to as the marriage syndrome. One spouse very much wants caritas and will be looking for signs that it is real.

There may be a definable set of circumstances in which sharing, or caritas in general, has a better chance to be fruitful rather than self-defeating. Namely, sharing with someone who is really looking for caritas and sharing that genuinely is caritas (it is harder to be caught faking if you are not faking) may be likely to have a benevolent effect. Someone who feels emotionally secure is not likely to be exploiting others for love. A securely well-fed person may be less likely to exploit the communal refrigerator. A financially secure person may be less likely to be exploitative regarding money. On the larger social scene, there might be an increase in caring and trust if people's felt needs were reduced, either by changing people's motivations or by satisfying them. If in our cities and suburbs the walls came down that separate the haves from the have-nots and goods and services were more equally shared, then theft might be less likely and trust might become more plausible.

The trouble is that boundaries may be necessary to permit the safe development of sharing. Consider a theoretical city with a transportation problem, namely very serious and chronic automobile congestion in a relatively small downtown area. Suppose further that the city tries to ameliorate the situation by urging people to use bicycles in this area. Bicycling is cheap, takes up little space, and is nonpolluting. There is a small difficulty that discourages people from using bicycles, namely that as soon as someone parks a bike someone else promptly steals it. Therefore, the city decides to take advantage of people's propensity for riding off with unattended bicycles. They create a large pool of communal bicycles to be left around on the streets for people to use as they wish. It is anticipated that at first people will steal these bicycles—that is, they will take them home and keep them from others' use—but that such stealing will cease when people realize it is pointless. There is almost always an adequate bicycle supply on the streets. Even the people who insist on having their own personal super-cycles will fear theft less as bicycle theft in general becomes less profitable.

Unfortunately, these rosy prospects may not come to pass. All we need assume is that there are other areas, such as in the suburbs or perhaps in other cities, in which bicycles retain substantial value, and that there are people around who are enterprising enough to acquire a few trucks. We can expect that the city will find that it is feeding bicycles into a bottomless pit of entrepreneurial bicycle theft. Unless the whole world changes simultaneously, completely open sharing is impossible without well-defended boundary conditions. If and only if there is some way to keep the bicycles in the defined downtown area, the communal bicycle plan might work. In fact, it is working every day, if we substitute cart for bicycle, and supermarket for downtown.

Thus we return to the basic set of contradictions or compromises that must be lived with if communes such as we have discussed, or aspects of them, are to endure or prosper. A group that insists on general sharing and mutual assistance, no hierarchical organization, and open boundaries is flirting with a short life expectancy. It is necessary to face the fact that an attitude of mutual sharing and trust requires real and perhaps well-defended boundary conditions, as in the hoary saying that there may be open towns with locked doors, or closed towns with open doors, but that there is a low survival rate for open towns with open doors.

Furthermore, some level of organization, and perhaps hierarchical organization, may be necessary in order to allocate unpopular but essential responsibilities and to defend boundaries. If an unpopular group is taken to court, it is helpful to make tactical decisions rapidly without an extended group process. Negotiations with parties outside the group may require the delegation of plenipotentiary authority to a few group members. When the police or the Hell's Angels come calling, or when a younger group member starts turning blue, a group meeting and consensus decision making may not be helpful.

Speculating on an ideal compromise arrangement is idle and beside the point. One central thesis that is very much not beside the point has something to do with the idea that compromise and flexibility have survival value. Ideological purity may be self-destructive even to the ideology in question. This thesis is actually a bit more specific than that. It is almost a paradoxical assertion concerning caritas. The conditions that may best permit caritas to begin and grow may be exactly those conditions that limit caritas, which use organizational or boundary restraints that essentially reduce the extent to which one can give or be taken from while getting nothing in return. Later, the situation seems to change, and some abandonment of limits, some leap of faith may be necessary if relationships are not to freeze in a compromise that is less than it could be. At first, however, it appears that caritas depends for its existence on the complementary existence of eros.

Passionate Love

Not only does the discussion of communes end with the odd assertion that caritas may, in some way or other, require eros; the very structure of the discussion contains this apparent contradiction. Caritas is characterized as a loving anarchy, and eros is tagged with the label of exploitation. Yet the discussion itself is addressed to a pragmatic question: If caritas is wanted, how can one be most likely to get it? While caritas is being lauded, the discussion itself approaches it from a wanting, from an eros point of view.

Now it is time for tables to be turned and for a more caritas-oriented attitude to be taken toward eros. If the preceding essay can be thought of as a pragmatist discussion of caritas, the present section can be thought of more as an appreciation of eros.

We turn back now to the subject of passionate love, or, to be more modest in objectives, let us say passionately romantic or even just romanticized involvement.

It is to be hoped that most intense romantic involvements include the warm and tender feelings associated with caring. There may be the seamless, global quality that has all aspects of the loved person—good, bad, or indifferent—equally treasured, if noticed. There may be a consuming, absorbing heightening of feeling in which the romantic involvement preempts other concerns and in which there is the tension of unfulfilled want.

The following little scene occured once while I was standing in line in a bakery, waiting to pay for some bagels. The scene included a cashier, one other employee of the bakery (the former were both male), two or three other customers in line, my young daughter (who was then aged 10), and myself. The second bakery employee said to the cashier that Fred, whoever he was, was not going to make it through the day. He went on to explain that Sue was away and not expected back until the next day. It was the first time she had been away. Fred had so far consumed several Valiums, but to no avail. He was simply not going to be able to make it. We all looked at each other and smiled indulgently. That is, we who for the most part had never seen each other before, who had not the slightest idea who Fred and Sue were, nonetheless felt that we understood enough of what was going on to adopt an attitude of benevolent amusement. Even my daughter smiled, and at the age of 10 her personal experience with consuming passion may have been limited. Somehow, an outsider finds something foolish, something silly about passionate feeling, and yet there is also something to be approved of, something attractive.

There is an old wartime anecdote that turns up from time to time, usually altered here and there to make it more topical. In this anecdote, a major surgical procedure has to be performed in the field without anesthetics. The patient, so it goes, expresses his thanks for the pain because it makes him aware that he is still alive. Perhaps passionate feeling can, in its own way, have some of the same quality of being both very painful and very alive.

Although intensely painful romantic feeling can be a consuming state, it is also thought usually to be a temporary one. Perhaps one reason it is temporary, if it is, is that people just cannot maintain indefinitely a consuming level of emotional intensity. I think, however, that although the surface intensity diminishes, buried frustration and want remain an enduring wound until and unless they are somehow satisfied. They may remain for a lifetime if there is no seized opportunity to finally satisfy the wanting.

When frustration continues, wanting (even if hidden) may go on. Tiring of the frustration and turning one's attention to other matters may feel better; but in the long run it may ensure that the frustration and want remain.

By the same token, continuation of intense want requires deprivation. Either the other person is (or seems to be) uncooperative, or there are external obstacles.

Historically, the idea of romance is based on the principle of want heightened by frustrating obstacles. Intensity builds until the obstacles are overcome or until the situation comes apart in some way, one fictional prototype being Romeo and Juliet. The cynical view that eros is the only love present may inform fictional outcomes in such popular works as *Gone With the Wind* or *Of Human Bondage*, in which the loved person is of no interest when he or she finally becomes available.

Some may remember Michelangelo Antonioni's classic film, *Blow Up*. In one scene its always distractable hero interrupts a chase to compete vigorously for a smashed guitar. After getting the guitar and walking outside with it, he glances idly at the guitar, drops it, and goes on his way.

The most pessimistic view of romance may be that of de Rougemont, cited earlier in this chapter. De Rougemont emphasizes that the story of Tristan and Isolde is (in the story's own words) a "high tale of love and death." In de Rougemont's view, a view most convenient for our practical-minded society, romance is nothing less than organized catastrophe, with death as its unspoken objective.

He is correct, of course, except that the full story is longer and does sometimes occur. Romance can lead to a leap from control, experienced as a kind of death (compare on a less dramatic scale the old view of orgasm as a soft death), followed by a kind of rebirth. This happens in romance labeled as such, and in the parallel experience to be found in therapy. Phenomenological reality must also be granted to the death and rebirth experience some find in religion, although most reports seem to suggest conventional rhetoric more than transformation of life.

One real-life pattern includes a rapid escalation of intensity and good feeling between two people, followed by a plateau in which it seems that a climactic event is about to happen. It does not. Then there is a slow decline in which one of the two acts deprived and frustrated and the other seems gradually to lose interest. If somewhere along the way the couple have become married, or have otherwise gotten themselves into a set of restraining circumstances, the decline may be stretched out indefinitely. This too has its parallel in therapy.

Looking beyond conscious and verbalized intentions, obstacles seem sometimes to be deliberately sought or created. Martin and Bird (1962) have called attention to the Oedipal aspect of a pattern in which people seem deliberately to seek an unattainable love object. There are also people who seem to become involved over and over in a pattern in which an apparently attainable love object is made unattainable by the emergence, either with or without apparent justification, of doubts, jealousy, and demandingness. Clearly for some, one purpose of involvement is to reinforce the relatively safe conviction that risk is unjustified, and to prove that one can flirt with danger without actually having to face success.

Acted-out doubts, jealousy, and demandingness and also actions that seem intended to incite these feelings in the other person, are mixed expressions of want, anger, and fear. They reflect at least some blend of yearning for the other person, fear of losing the other person, bitterness at not having completely attained the other person's love, and fear that the other person might be more available than is safe.

Somehow, the tenderness, yearning, and fear that is in this mix, the vulnerability of it, is often barely visible behind the much more open display of anger and resentful demands that themselves might be hidden behind a mask of unconcern. Negative feelings protect one from vulnerability (both felt and real); but without the emergence of vulnerability there may be no satisfaction of wanting. Painful as it may feel, this course must often not seem as painful, frightening, or self-destructive as the risk of open vulnerability.

If the more painful aspects of passionate involvement depend partly on being deprived, they should be related not only to unconscious or unspoken wishes that can be traced back to one's childhood, but also to external circumstances. It should be possible, and of course it is, to document cases in which enforced separations, parental hostility, and other obstacles seem to have fueled these aspects (Driscoll, Davis, & Lipetz, 1972). It should also be possible to look at a series of courtships and to see whether losses, when they occur, seem sometimes to have been initiating factors. Such seems to be the case (Jacobson & Ryder, 1969; Hepworth, Ryder, & Dreyer, 1984).

Fortunately or unfortunately, obstacles to loving relationships appear to be readily available, and everyone experiences losses. Erotic romance, with and without pain, with and without exhilaration, is very much with us. I think, or at least I hope, that there are few people whose lives are totally untouched by it. The bite of passionate feeling, when and if it occurs, can be welcomed and can be seen as reminding us that we are capable of feeling intensely alive.

Virtue

Virtue? Bad enough to talk of how to permit the existence of caritas and worse to openly express positive feelings toward eros; but surely some sort of pale has been passed, some minimum of self-restraint has been dropped, if we are to discuss something called virtue. At the least we should write it in quotes and carefully explain that what we are discussing is not *really* virtue but some subtle, more scientific equivalent. Unfortunately, to ignore the idea of virtue is to ignore an important aspect of over two thousand years of thought on the subject of love. In a way, a discussion of caritas is by definition a discussion of virtue, just as platonism seems often to have been used in a denial of virtue, or to deal with virtue indirectly (with the idea that enlightened selfishness turns out ultimately to be virtuous).

Even in the present discussion, caring has been described in terms of bread cast upon the waters. One trusts that ultimately, eventually, indirectly, and possibly, the bestowal will return. One hopes, or perhaps it is more accurate to say that one has faith, that the expression of caring will ultimately help to satisfy wanting.

However, even to state that relationship so directly compromises caritas and moves it closer in appearance to eros. The distinction is not one of abstract philosophizing, but concrete, down-to-earth experience. Consider again the marriage syndrome. Any attempts to satisfy the demands of the more overtly demanding spouse are doomed to failure as long as the attempts are made in response to the demands, and do not provide the bestowal of caring that is the one thing that can be given only voluntarily.

Setting effective deception to one side, activities have the possibility of effectively reducing demands only if not done for the purpose of reducing demands. They must express caritas. They must express, that is, feeling that is not directed toward any immediate, or direct, or even certain reward. Anyone caring for another person and expressing it in such a situation should be aware that an indirect benefit may be very indirect and that *eventually* may mean *never*.

It has become a clinical commonplace that one person's attempts to force another to change can be the chief obstacle to change. If the spouse of a heavy drinker really gives up on trying to get the drinker to change, is willing to love the person as is, then the drinker might change. Or might not.

Thus, the word *virtue*, in this context, refers to something very specific. It refers to those ways of acting the only immediate justification for which can be that they are genuine, or appropriate, or good—in a word, that they are virtuous—because they neither guarantee nor make highly likely any immediate benefit whatever. The best that can be said for such actions, from a self-oriented point of view, is that they permit at least the possibility of close human relationships and that in the long run one may have reason to be glad about having done these things. Immediately and in the short run, from a hard headed, realistic, or cynical point of view, the only rational justification for such actions is virtue or caring. Oh yes, there is also the possibility that one will feel good about oneself being brave or honest enough to be vulnerable, or for caring enough to expose the depth of one's wants.

In recent years there seems to have been a certain amount of interest in interpersonal skills, in teaching people how to communicate, how to break down restrictive barriers between people, how to generate relationships that are more real or meaningful. A suspicious person might see in these efforts the intention to use particularly clever tricks to eliminate trickery and to manipulate people into being less controlling. An interest in skills may partly reflect a retreat from the embarrassing subject of virtue. It was popular for a while, for example, to believe that people should be direct, immediate, and "up front," and so the propensity for being that way was referred to as a skill. Perhaps it is a skill; but I think it would have been more accurate (and more up front) to call it a virtue.

Candor is, I think, a primary particular virtue in interpersonal relationships. The reference here is not necessarily to baring all the facts of one's history or other involvements, but to being honest and open, being real, in the present tense fact of a relationship, even if it seems not in one's interest. In the short run, and in terms of practical considerations, candor can be inconvenient, a nuisance, or not worth the trouble. It really guarantees nothing except perhaps some intense or uncomfortable interaction. Yet, as I understand the word *candor*, and as I understand what an intimate relationship is, the latter is impossible without the former. Far from being a skill, candor may require the deliberate sacrifice of interpersonal skills.

A young woman, a client, once confided to me that she had made careful advance plans to marry her future husband. She had arranged to meet him in some casual setting, and, so she boasted, had managed to get him into bed with her in 20 minutes flat. Twenty minutes is not a world's record by any means, but she was pleased with it. It was a skillful and successful opening gambit in a strategy that had them in short order at the altar. Why was she telling me all this?

The woman was providing background material in the hope that I would then be better able to help her with her marital problem. Her marital complaint was that her husband did not love her very much. She felt that he was never interested in her except for sex.

Whatever caring another person comes to feel, if any, can only be caring for what one has seemed to be. Exactly to the extent that one is successful in fooling people, or keeping from them unpleasant personal aspects, one is successful at best in having people care about what one is not. If that is satisfactory, then all well and good. Otherwise, candor is a logical necessity.

A husband and wife crab and complain at each other. Nothing either one does is satisfying to the other. Then in what feels like one clear moment of truth, one of them says, "Don't you realize that I love you desperately, and I am terrified that you may not love me as much? Please care about me." The other spouse hears and reaches out. Complaints and demandingness return later. There has been no miracle. But there has been a change, and the relationship becomes more tender.

In this example, directness and candor occur as a kind of dyadic version of therapeutic intepretation. Camouflage is lifted from a truth, followed by a restructuring of the interpersonal dynamics. (Or is it the restructuring, already in process, that has produced the apparent "intervention"?)

People who say that they are particularly honest often mean that they are indiscriminately unkind to people. This is no virtue. Here, candor refers to a more tender honesty, and as such it seems almost a logical necessity for caritas. This is not to suggest that honesty causes caring, although that might sometimes be possible. More plausibly, caring causes honesty.

There is also one other particular virtue I would like to mention, and it is related to candor. It is simply to take seriously the possibility of accepting other people at face value, at least on occasion, when there is no convincing reason to believe them. Without a willingness to accept that others' statements mean just what they seem to mean, it becomes difficult to receive or even to hear the gift of caring. With this willingness, one may or may not receive a gift, but one is certainly giving one.

It is the difference between trusting and entrusting. If a person wishes to borrow money from you, and you loan the person the money, you might do so without really trusting that the person will return it. But nonetheless you might entrust the person with some of your money. Relationships grow when there are extensions of the self beyond what is safe, and beyond what is assured. To be more exact, they do not grow when such extensions do not occur.

Final Note

One thing is clear. From the point of view of a dry-minded Platonist, there is plenty of reason to shy away from caritas and the distinction between eros and caritas. Even romance is a problem. It is not so bad if eros tends to enter into a discussion of caritas, but if caritas tends to enter into a discussion of eros, one can be cornered into a consideration of caring, and even, God forbid, of virtue. Having gotten that far, one is certainly outside of science.

Perhaps, however, being outside of science is not the worst of fates. It might even be possible to reenter the field of descriptive investigation with a little bit better idea of what is going on. Admitting the reality of caring is required if one is to describe or even to think about describing events as they are. To see a distinction between eros and caritas may be a way to understand some clearly empirical, and not easily wished-away phenomena, and perhaps also a way for the researcher to think about his or her own work.

The idea, finally, is not to suggest that one kind of feeling, or one kind of approach to feelings, is better than the other. Eros and caritas correspond to two ways of feeling, and to two ideologies about all feeling. However, I suggest that to take either of these viewpoints seriously requires taking them both seriously. One then must make choices.

The last section, in discussing substrate versus intentionality, contrasted two extreme views of the therapist vis-à-vis the client or client party. One view emphasized a substrate view of the client(s) but with the therapist seen as more of an intentional being, not so much as a clockwork orange.

Here the contrast is not quite the same. The client or client party may well be thought of as intentional and in that sense human, but with the therapist as somehow above the clients' humanity. This is the extreme Platonist view. A client is seen as a struggling mortal, and the therapist—while in that role—as an essentially unmoved mover. To a far greater extent than the client, the therapist is untouched by the therapeutic events. The therapist may be paid to touch people emotionally, but not to be touched.

The other extreme is clear. Therapists and clients become fellow strugglers, with the risks and opportunities of change, hurt and benefit shared on both sides. A therapist with this view might argue that no client ever changes profoundly who is not loved. The therapist is paid to take a leap of fortune with a stranger, or group of strangers, and to be prepared to accept the risks involved. It is not quite that the therapist is paid to care, since that would be literally a contradiction in terms. The distinction is subtle enough to invite cynicism: The therapist cares, and therefore should be paid.

This is not the place to discuss therapist honesty, but it should be mentioned that many therapists seem to have a Platonist view while pretending that they actually join their clients in their struggles. The long-range consequences of this pretense, if it becomes part of therapists' public image, seem likely to be fairly negative. The choice in research is less noticeable, but if it can be imagined, a continuum does exist going from eros to caritas.

Over and over, one is faced not just with the choice of whether to study love from an eros or caritas point of view—whether to see love as eros or as caritas or some blend, but whether to express one or the other of these views in the research itself. Does one approach phenomena from the point of view of how to make them happen, how to fix them, how to get desired things from them, or does one approach them from the point of view of curiosity and benevolence? The question is whether one looks at the world and sees levers to pull to get what one wants or looks at the world and sees beauty—in a sense bestows beauty. The former approach, if successful, might be profitable. The latter approach, if successful, might feel good.

III

GOALS TO BE RELINQUISHED

7

CAUSALITY

People have done research to find out why the grass is green or the sky blue, why children smile or adults go crazy, and why married couples get divorced. "Why"—the general idea of causality—seems to have been used in a variety of different ways, leading to some potential confusion about what all this work might mean or could mean. It has been recognized at least since Aristotle's time that causality could mean several things, or equivalently that there might be several kinds of causality. In social science the existence of this variety has not been much honored. At the same time, differing usages have actually been employed. There is, of course, the idea of necessary and sufficient antecedents based strictly on demonstrated facts. There are also usages that relate more closely to animism, moral judgment, or both. Animism is the one I like best.

The very idea of "usage" depends not so much on particular assertions made as on the intentions that these assertions seem to reveal. But then the idea of "intention" involves the view that there is an imagined entity lying behind what is most visible and somehow resulting in the events that outsiders can perceive directly. This is what is meant here by animism, that one constructs a myth of an entity not immediately seen, that "causes" what is seen, and that is invested with a life of its own. It is not that strange, after all, to imagine that behind the visible surface of a person's life there is a private person who is in some sense more fundamental than what shows. Most conceptualizing in social science is of this form. An explanatory concept of some sort, a mythology, is invented, and then is so loved by its inventor that it seems to have life and to be real, at least to the inventor. There may not be that much difference in this regard between those who write clinical, humanistically oriented mythologies and those who spell out more rigidly logical or mathematical views. The primary meaning of cause in this context seems thus to be the command structure between the myth and what is observed. There are three aspects to this kind of cause that might usefully be distinguished.

First, from a phenomenological point of view, myth has sometimes been created out of what was once perception. As ordinary citizens, we see and hear a person, recognize certain of that person's intentions, and probably regard him or her as a more or less whole human being. When we approach a similar person with the scientific attitude, so to speak, of trying to be totally objective, all we can see is behavior. We school ourselves not to accept our naive perception of a whole person. After we do that, we then create a myth to stand behind the behavior (whether the myth is thought of as a person, as some collection of neural linkages, or whatever) to replace what we discarded when we stopped being naive.

Thus scientific objectivity creates a need for imagination and fantasy. It is an open question whether dividing what is observed into outer and inner entities is always more useful than the more innocent view that an organic whole is more or less directly perceived. Perhaps the worst outcome is that some people become radical "outerists" and go through their professional careers claiming to see nothing but outer manifestations (of what?), and swearing that the tip of the iceberg is all the iceberg there is.[1]

Most social scientists can make a pretty decent guess about how people will act in a given setting. Partly this knowledge comes just from living in the same society as the persons being studied and partly it comes from such organized professional activities as exploratory work or pretesting. Partly also it comes from being the sort of person who is interested in what people do. After all, none of us got into this trade purely by accident. Given this professional skill, the second notable aspect of animistic causality follows logically from the fact that causal myths are largely products of the imagination. Whether unwittingly or deliberately, causal myths can be treated readily as if they were taffy. They can be stretched out to predict what is already expected to happen. The fact that what is predicted actually occurs can then be used as a confirmation of the conceptual framework.

To judge from informal comments heard from time to time, one common complaint about social science is that it regularly proves the obvious. To the extent that this complaint has any validity, it seems likely that investigators are not so much interested in the observed phenomena per se, as in showing that some conceptualization yields correct predictions. Such predictions (of things that might be predicted without the conceptualization) do enhance the value of conceptual views that support the predictions, but only by way of showing that the conceptual views *encompass* phenomena that already, more or less, are believed to occur. They are not really predictions in the sense of suggesting an empirical fact that is not presently known.

Conceptual mythologies of one sort or another are probably a permanent and necessary fact of life, and may be helpful and interesting devices for organizing a range of phenomena, including phenomena that are expected to happen in the future. They may even lead to altered expectations of events not yet perceived, which would be very nice indeed. However, the organization of predictions that would be made anyway is best not confused with making changed predictions on the basis of a conceptualization. The former is silver, but the latter is gold.

The third notable aspect of causal animism is that cause is likely to refer to a logical or quasi-logical relationship, rather than to a temporal sequence of physical events. Charlie is terrified of being best at something, therefore he misses a lot of easy baskets when his team is too far ahead. The "therefore" in this expression is a causality that either means logical implication, or something close to it, and expresses a relationship between cause and effect that has no necessary time dimension [compare Rychlak's (1977) discussion of "formal" cause]. To put it another way, "cause" in this context is not very distinct from a noncausal way of speaking, as in the view that Charlie's fears are regularly *expressed* by missing easy shots, or even the view that what we *mean* by Charlie's alleged fears is a congeries of actions that occasionally includes becoming an incompetent basketball player. To put it still another way, cause in this context is itself part of the conceptual myth, and may best be thought of as metaphor, that may or may not be compelling to one's imagination. This quasi-logical, quasi-definitional linkage between allegedly underlying concept and observed behavior is very different from the event sequence interpretation of causality, in which, say, my finger strikes a key and thus causes a typewriter to print a letter.

Animistic causality can of course mean nothing more than summarizing a set of observations by giving them a name and then investing the name itself with a life of its own. If the observed facts already have a name, they can be renamed, and the second name can be the one given life, and used to explain the first. This can be most easily illustrated by an animistic renaming that almost no one would actually do these days. Suppose a person's activity seems well described by saying that the person is sleepy almost all the time. The sleepiness is then "explained" by inventing a property that "causes" sleepiness, let us say "soporific propensity" or SP. Since SP does nothing else but cause something that is only a summary label for observations, and has no obvious claim to being anything other than an alternative summary label, it can be said that SP is a pure case of an animistic and vacuous usage of causality. Its total function is to stand behind what has already been described without adding anything to the description.

More realistic examples are necessarily less clear-cut, since anyone who invents causal explanations must believe them to be less than vacuous. Consider a man who regularly acts in the ways that clinicians are likely to describe as obsessional. Having thus described what he does, is something added by saying that he *is* an obsessional personality type? Is a habitual drunk better explained by being called an alcoholic? Maybe the answer to questions like these is, necessarily, maybe.

Why does Joe sleep with men? Because he is gay, you dummy. Oh, I see.

Again, the problem with formulations that may be vacuously animistic has nothing to do with particular terms, such as type, alcoholic, or gay, but with one of the ways such terms can be used. Not much is gained simply by using a term to stand behind the attributes it seems to summarize, as if the label caused the attributes.

The animistic use of labels is equally possible when data is quantitative and electronically processed. If a factor, which is totally defined by observed relationships, is in turn said to "explain" these same relationships, little or nothing may have been added to the bare empirical facts except that some aspects of these facts have been invested, vacuously, with a life of their own. Once more, however, the quarrel is not with particular words, but with uses to which they might be put. "Explain," after all, could be used in no sense but the narrow, statistical one of how much variance is encompassed in a factor.

In the broad universe of real and potential sin, it must be said that vacuously animistic "causal" explanations are about as minor as you can get. For the most part their worst cost is that they can introduce a little confusion. Sometimes, though, an explanation is almost vacuous but conveys implications, almost covertly, that may not be desirable. A psychiatric diagnosis, for example, can follow one through life, with the twin implications that the label applied refers to relatively permanent (undesirable) attributes, and that the attributes referred to are somehow a fundamental aspect of the person who gets to bear the label. Thus we slide from causality construed as animism to causality as blame, since a diagnosis is readily used both as animistic cause and as something to blame for a person's sorry or offensive life.

Causality as moral judgment is difficult to avoid when the phenomena to be explained are heavily value laden. Consider Dray's (1962) discussion of historical causality in the context of the American Civil War. He concludes that there can be no objective, well-defined answer to the question of who or what caused the war. The problem he points to is not that the causal network is so complex or subtle but that the question is usually posed in what turns out to be a moral context. It is not, "what were the necessary and sufficient antecedents," but, "who or what was to *blame* for the war."

Nature versus Nurture debates can be partially understood in the same way. The "schizophrenogenic" mother, or family, is in part someone or something to blame, to be held responsible for a child's unhappiness. But if schizophrenia is inherited, then the mother and the rest of the family can rest easy, secure in the knowledge that they are not to blame. Similarly, if environment causes blacks to get lower scores on performance tests, then the white population must be held responsible. But if there are lower scores due to genetic factors, then the white population can continue discriminatory practices in good conscience, or at least this line of argument seems implicit in these controversies.

For those of us who work professionally with married couples in the process of becoming formerly married, cause as blame can loom large. Blame, in fact, can look like the only kind of cause to be found. By the same token, a clear conceptual shift can sometimes be seen when clients notice that other ways of understanding their predicament may be more enlightening.

Scientists and clinicians are not embittered spouses, or if they are, they try to transcend that unpleasant fact in their professional work. Although scientists and clinicians usually do not like to think of their professional work as expressing blame, it can readily happen by inadvertence. If a historian claims to disavow passing judgment, but evinces utter conviction that the North really did cause the Civil War, she or he might at least agree that the North is not being paid a compliment.

Certain clues of blame can sometimes be found lurking in a causal framework alleged to be impartial. It is obvious that fairly similar kinds of things can be described either in positive ways or in negative ones. The tone of the terms used changes as the hats worn change from white to black. Perseverance is different (is it?) from perseveration or rigidity.

Flexibility is different, maybe, from inconsistency. Interactional skill is different from being manipulative, on occasion. Usually, when causality is used in the sense of passing judgment, the tone of the alleged cause is consistent with the tone of the alleged result. It is never the good guys who are said to have caused the Civil War. No one has been thought to have become schizophrenic because the person's parents were too loving and kind. No, if a person comes to grief in some way, it is because of a fatal flaw or weakness, or because nearby people have behaved badly. In general, disability is not seen as the result of virtue.

Out in the real world, if it is organized by an impersonal nature rather than by a meta-moralistic deity, there must be situations in which noble or competent acts or attributes are the necessary or sufficient antecedents of catastrophe. If something like this comes to our attention, it is easy to turn it rapidly into more familiar but less positive terms. Suppose parents love a child so much, or are so kind to the child, that the child is hopelessly disadvantaged when faced with the nastier world outside the home. It only takes a moment's reflection to conclude that these parents are in actuality doing no kindness to their child, that they are overprotective, probably clinging, and maybe a bit on the schizoid side. The "love" they express is likely to be relabeled in less attractive terms. If these parents decide to avoid catastrophe for their child by keeping the child indefinitely in the warm and loving home environment, perhaps plus some other environments that they can control well, the results might be better for the child or less good. If better, observers might describe them in positive terms, but if less good, the parents might risk really severe condemnation in labels, not to mention the possibility of legal action.

The third usage of causality to be discussed is the one that is thought to be a matter of empirical demonstration, at least in principle—that is, cause as being a necessary and sufficient antecedent of that which is caused. It is difficult to imagine speculation about important events without the speculation including ideas of causality in this present sense. Causal speculation can be fascinating and intellectually compelling. Apparent causal demonstrations also can be fascinating, but they are unlikely to be very compelling. There are several reasons for this.

Let us imagine a large jar of marbles, each of which represents a situation in which causal demonstration would be desirable. Let us stipulate that for each of these marbles the alleged cause to be studied is something of some real human importance. Is it bad for a marriage to marry someone from another ethnic group? Is parenting different as a consequence of how many children one has? Does day care over a period of time warp a child's development? Allegedly causal manipulations that are relatively trivial from a human point of view, as in a study, say, of the short term effect of clothing style on rated attractiveness, are excluded. Each marble thus represents a desired causal demonstration, and each alleged cause is a variable that, by definition, might have a serious effect on people. It will turn out that some marbles represent situations in which a causal demonstration is impossible. If all these latter marbles are removed from the jar, how many are left?

Many, perhaps even most of the marbles are removed just because of current thinking about how causality works. Few people believe that uncomplicated, linear causality, involving only one cause and one effect, actually exists in most social science situations. It is more common to believe that a large and complex collection of variables or entities mutually affect each other in causal systems. These systems may be impossible to disentangle even speculatively, much less empirically. Different events may be thought of as having similar consequences or as contributing to each other's consequences. Any given event may be thought of as having consequences that are conditional on a large array of circumstances. Given this degree of complexity in what is imagined to exist, the design of an experiment that will demonstrate it is quite difficult to imagine.

Still, some marbles are left in the jar. There are situations in which people believe in linear causality and that seem less susceptible to mind-blocking complications. Effectiveness of psychotherapy (or family therapy, marriage enrichment, or some other "treatment") is such a situation, in that two rather remarkable positions are taken. Namely, psychotherapy (or some particular brand of it) is thought to be a single entity, as aspirin is thought to be a single entity, and causality, if any, is thought to be in a single direction.

Let us imagine an experiment designed to test the effectiveness of psychotherapy. There will be a variable manipulated independently—that is, an independent variable—and some set of variables the values of which might depend on the experimental manipulations—that is, a set of dependent variables. The first problem will be to define psychotherapy, and this will not be a trivial matter. For present purposes, however, it will be assumed that an acceptable definition is reached, and that other "merely" substantive problems are resolved. Notably, a set of dependent variables is identified that is psychometrically reasonable and that also satisfies the ideologies and epistemologies of the therapists and researchers involved. Perhaps it is obvious that in an actual study these substantive problems would probably be very difficult to resolve. The reason for dismissing them so readily here is to get on with suggesting that there are general problems with this kind of demonstration, not limited to any particular subject matter, as long as the independent variable is thought capable of having serious effects on people.

As any advanced college student knows, the first order of business is to provide or not provide treatment strictly on the basis of chance. A person's location in the experimental or control group should be on the basis of a purely random decision process. Good luck. The fact is, and probably should be, that if there are two treatments—for example, therapy and control—and if many people believe that one of them is much more helpful than the other, it will be very difficult to get support for denying the allegedly better treatment to a random subset of subjects totally without regard for their condition. Social scientists just do not have a license for playing with people's lives in this way. Therefore, for lack of funds, legal clearances, or some other necessary social support, many more marbles must be taken from the jar. In effect, an experimental demonstration is defeated by ethical considerations.

Consider the marbles left. In some way or another, support is acquired for strict random assignment. Funds are obtained, legal clearances are obtained, and serious dissent is mollified. The next problem is likely to be that the subjects of this research are people, not white rats. When they do not like what is happening they have a distressing habit of taking a walk. The drop-out problem in studies of this kind does not seem amenable to any easy solution and is probably fatal to the logic of the intended causal demonstration. Note that dropouts occur in the experimental group as well as in the control group. There seems to be no happy way to deal with a person who drops out, say, after the second therapy session. If such a person is counted as a member of the experimental group, it seems "unfair" to psychotherapy to expect it to have an effect so rapidly, and posttesting is probably not feasible anyway. If the person is simply eliminated from the study, there are other problems.

Assume that therapy does absolutely nothing but that on a strictly random basis some clients get better over time and others get worse. If dropouts from the experimental group are systematically more likely to be from among the clients who are getting worse (and it is hard to see how this possibility can be proven wrong), removing these clients from the study will make the experimental group look more improved. Using analogous reasoning, controls, who may be sitting on a waiting list, might be more likely to drop out if they get better. Their motivation for waiting around, by this line of thought, is reduced if they improve spontaneously. Thus removing control group dropouts from the study may make the control group look more as if it is getting worse. Such a study will "show" that therapy is more effective than the control condition, even though there is no real effect of therapy whatsoever. If an investigator cannot prove that suppositions such as these are untrue, it may be impossible to show that an apparent demonstration of therapeutic effectiveness is really what it seems to be.

By definition, members of a control group are not being treated, even though they may want treatment. Inevitably, some of these persons must be uncooperative enough to seek treatment elsewhere, whether it is formally defined as such or not. An experimenter may not even find out that this is going on, with the effect that resulting data become misleading.

Generalizing from the dropout problem, and the semi-dropout problem of people finding alternative treatments for themselves, it is probably true that even with nominally total power to assign people to experimental or control groups, people are likely to seek (and to find) ways in which they can choose for themselves whether or not they will be, or stay, in some particular group. Once experimental subjects are self-selecting their own experimental treatment conditions, there is no longer random assignment to conditions, and no longer an experimental demonstration of cause and effect. Exit more marbles.

Still another unpleasant aspect of the real world is that even if people do not drop out of a study, they may or may not remain friendly. Worse, a client's attitude may be systematically related to membership in the experimental or control group. Friendliness or animosity, alas, can have a substantial and perhaps fatal effect on the quality of data obtained. Exit still more marbles.

It may be no exaggeration to suggest that the number of marbles remaining in the jar at this point is quite small, although some situations certainly remain in which causal demonstrations might be feasible.

To pursue the therapy problem, one potentially feasible approach might be to compare treatments that seem of roughly equal value both to granting agencies and to potential clients. The catch-22 is of course that in so doing, the investigator is more likely to have two treatments that *do* have roughly equal effects (on the dependent variables measured), with obvious but depressing consequences. Another possibility is to study a genuinely captive group of people, such as inpatients, or to use dependent variables that are insensitive to subjects' attitudes toward treatment, yet somehow sensitive to what the treatment is supposed to do. Perhaps such measures as gainful employment in the next X months, or five-year rate of readmissions, fall into this category. One whole class of studies that is not subject to many of the problems mentioned is so-called experiments of nature. Plausibly random fate may have selected persons to receive one or another "treatment." For example, there might be a study on the effect of the first child's gender on marital interaction, based on the assumption that for all practical purposes gender is a random event. A study of the effects of parental loss might work, if the parents in question were lost by death, and if it were assumed that the deaths were in no way caused by anything that could be related more directly to any dependent variables. A study of the effects of parental loss by divorce would most likely *not* work, since events leading to the divorce are likely to be plausibly related to many events of interest happening later, independently of the divorce. That is, divorce is less plausible as a genuine independent variable.

For the most part, experimental causal demonstrations are extremely likely to founder, either on ethical restrictions as to what can be done or will be supported, or on the practical difficulties of trying to treat people like laboratory animals when actually one has far from total control over them. It is doubtful that a white rat has ever bribed a research assistant to switch its experimental treatment group, but from what I have heard, even this has happened in studies involving people.

If one adds to these problems the unpleasant fact that most measurement procedures available are outrageously blunt instruments, it becomes readily understandable that well-designed and well-executed causal demonstrations are almost—but not quite—as scarce as unicorns.

The evaluation of psychotherapy has been thought to have such social importance that there has been support for experimentation that is almost unique in social science, yet even here almost all the research attempts have failed. That they have not demonstrated the effectiveness of psychotherapy is largely true but not necessarily a research failure. The significant fact is that they have generally failed to bring off an accomplished experiment that has the methodological soundness to really demonstrate whether psychotherapy does or does not do anything (forgetting about whether or not what it does is desirable).

What it comes down to is that for most practical purposes, causal demonstrations involving variables that might have serious effects on people are close to impossible. Social scientists are a plucky lot, and not always deterred by simple impossibility. Thus three main strategies have been adopted to deal with this inconvenient reality.

First, there is simple recourse to magic. One picks two variables and just decides to regard one of them as independent, the other, of course, being regarded as dependent. For example, one may observe that couples marrying across ethnic boundaries are more likely to get divorced, and conclude that couples marrying across ethnic boundaries are *therefore* more likely to get divorced. Alternative interpretations are ignored, such as the possibility that people unconventional enough to marry across ethnic boundaries may also have unconventional ideas about the necessity for enduring marriage. As Bell (1968) has pointed out, observed correlations between parent attributes and child attributes have often been interpreted, gratuitously, to mean that the parent attributes *caused* the child ones. Other interpretations, as Bell also noted, might have been equally likely.

A second strategy is to use surrogate variables. One may not be able to manipulate passionate love, but perhaps an experimental manipulation of mild liking is possible. One can then assume that what is true for mild liking is also true for passionate love. It is hoped that one cannot manipulate choice of marriage partners, but perhaps choice of dancing partners at a college dance can be managed successfully. One can then try to generalize from dancing partnerships to more serious relationships.

A third strategy is to get complicated. A simple correlation between X and Y might have fairly obvious multiple interpretations, but if there is a complicated set of correlations involving X, Y, and a dozen other variables, alternative explanations become more difficult. In effect, a causal interpretation might be accepted due to a failure of imagination. In path analysis, a set of relationships is examined to see if they are consistent with some proposed causal model. If consistency is found, it might then be argued that the causal model has become more plausible, although of course not proven. It seems to me that such a conclusion is probably imprudent if the model is not compared to some alternative model that may not be causal and that also may be consistent with obtained relationships. Another way to look at the effectiveness of path analysis would be to try it with models that are known to be false. For example, one could examine the consistency of obtained relationships with a causal model of interest, and then examine consistency with the same model, but with time running backward. My guess is that in some analyses (Tessor & Paulhus, 1976) an impossible model may look almost as good as the one the investigator would like to support.

In general, correlational information does not turn into proof of causality just by being complicated. Although accepting a particular model (causal or otherwise) because alternative explanations cannot be imagined might be justified on occasion, there may be plenty of occasions in which this failure of imagination says more about the investigator than about the subject of the investigation.

Each of these alternative strategies has at least one strength, which is that much interesting information might be gathered, even if convincing evidence of causality is not. Furthermore, it is imaginable that the use of surrogate variables, or some really decisively complex network of correlational relationships, might be really convincing as evidence of some causal view. Although this may be unlikely, it is at least possible.

Suppose that an investigator does succeed at an experimental demonstration of causality, actually manipulating an independent variable that is demonstrated to have a nontrivial effect on human beings. Frightening as this possibility may be (at least to this author), it may nonetheless fail to achieve what the investigator actually wants to demonstrate. A study of psychotherapy may be for the purpose of learning what *can* change people, but a study of successful and unsuccessful marriages may be intended for the purpose of learning what ordinarily *does* cause success or failure. Difficult as it might be to learn about "can," it is tougher to learn about "does." To take a simple example not involving people, an investigator may be able to demonstrate that some experimentally controlled pattern of reinforcement leads pigeons to fight—in the research laboratory. This is not a demonstration that the pigeons one sees fighting in the park do so for the same reasons. In other words, the form of experimentation that is customary for demonstrating causality is adequate only for demonstrating that an independent variable is a *sufficient* antecedent of a dependent variable, but is not up to the task of showing that the independent variable is a *necessary* antecedent, and may say little about what usually happens out in the real, not *experimental*, world.

Causal speculation is probably inevitable, and explanatory mythologies involving the concept of cause in one way or another can be fascinating and plausible. However, anyone who wishes to take causality seriously as an object of empirical investigation, and who is interested in things that may have serious effects on people's lives, is likely to experience serious difficulties. It may not be worth the candle to spend a significant portion of someone's career, or a significant portion of the professional talent generally available, on empirical investigations designed to demonstrate what causes what. Causality seems to be discussed widely in research literature as if it were what we are all after. The truth is to the contrary, that in general its pursuit is only slightly less futile than the pursuit of the Holy Grail, unless we are willing to spend our time studying the ephemeral effects of variables we are able to study because it is already believed that their effects are ephemeral.

Note

1. The view here is similar to something Roszak (1972) says about science in general. He suggests that Christian theology effectively sold the idea of a universe made up of the mundane, which is only mud, and the supernatural, in which all that is really precious resides. Atheistic science, according to Roszak, has kept the same basic idea but rejected the existence of the supernatural, concluding of course that reality is only mud.

8

OBJECTIVITY AND BEHAVIOR

Objectivity is desirable in moderation. Overdone, it can cause blindness to such things as subtleties, woods as opposed to trees, entities that can be known only by inference, and that slippery attribute called "meaning." If objectivity is sought by studying only behavior, excessive operational concreteness results in studying things that have less clear meaning and that are less interesting. Generally speaking, behavior as such is not particularly interesting stuff. Perhaps it might be advisable to pay it less attention and to pay more attention to other things.

What other things? What, after all, is there to observe besides behavior? "Behavior" seems to be one of those terms with a definition that can expand or contract depending on the purposes to which it is put. "Marriage" and "family" are also terms of this sort. For example, to advance an argument that marriage is a universal institution in all known human societies, a fairly broad definition of marriage is desirable. An argument may then go on to state that since marriage is universal, it would be dangerous and unwise to try to get rid of it (or to do things that would be tantamount to getting rid of it). Almost certainly this last sentence implies a definition of marriage that is much more narrow than in the sentence immediately preceding it. Why worry about attempts to get rid of something that is defined so broadly that it cannot be gotten rid of?

Similarly, if a science of behavior is to include everything that might be interesting, it makes sense to speak of behavior in a very general sense so as to leave nothing out. On the other hand, if the virtues of behavioral objectivity are to be extolled, as contrasted with less concrete phenomena, some shrinkage in definition is desirable.

According to the broadest definition, behavior includes everything people do that is observable, plus some other things. The concept of internal and invisible behavior is surely troubling if the virtue of behaviorism is its objectivity, but it is nonetheless true that references have been made to such entities. The earliest one that I know of is Clark Hull's (1933) borrowing (without citation) of Bernheim's psychomotor concept and referring in that context to pure stimulus acts. These invisible acts had no effect but to stimulate other acts.

It is possible to take the view that the study of external behavior might be informative about internal and invisible behavior, or even the stronger position that internal behavior must operate according to the same rules as the external variants. Observation of what is visible can then be used in lieu of observing what is not visible. Fine as this formulation might be, it does not refer only to facts that can be directly and objectively observed. This broad definition of behavior could be used in a scientific endeavor that is nonetheless objective, or as objective as any such endeavor, but the objectivity of such an effort would not be a consequence of it being behavior that is studied.

An all-encompassing definition of behavior presents problems apart from questions of objectivity. If behavior means everything, it means nothing. It is pointless to urge that people study behavior instead of something else if there is nothing else. If the definition could be narrowed down to mean all that is objectively observable, would any other observable things—not behavior—be left out? For now, we will define behavior as meaning any human activity that is directly observable. This second definition will present problems in due course.

Operational definition used to be much valued as a way to achieve objectivity, even though terms might be used that sounded like wishy-washy, hard-to-define internal states. Now, to be strict about it, no operational definitions have ever been actually established since Percy Bridgman (1927) laid down impossible criteria. The idea was that a variable was completely defined by a complete specification of the operations used to measure it, including specification of the values of all other pertinent variables at the time of measurement. That last phrase kills it, because it means that all other pertinent variables have to be known, and measured (presumably according to their own operational definitions), before an operational definition for any given variable can be specified. All variables, or at least many of them, must be well measured before any variable can be well measured, on top of which the relationships among variables have to be known (to establish pertinence) before they can be defined.

Within psychology these minor quibbles did not seem very troubling. In the heyday of this sort of thing, one might have said simply that intelligence was defined as score on such and such a test or that manifest anxiety was defined as such and such a test score. Operational definition, used in this way, could be a gesture toward objectivity that permitted unwarranted and subjective generalizations to be offered without plausible argument. One could not argue with an operational definition. It was whatever the author said it was. But when the discussion section of a paper was reached, "Intelligence" or "Manifest Anxiety" (both carefully defined to *mean* particular test scores), might be replaced by intelligence and anxiety (both defined not at all). Presto, generalizations about subjects of great interest (unobjective as they might be) could be generated just by dropping initial capital letters.

Such clumsy use of operational definition would be unlikely today. It is interesting now only as a way that manifest objectivity can facilitate generalizations that might not really be objectively supportable. More important at the moment is the question of whether, say, intelligence defined as a particular test score fits the definition of behavior offered earlier.

There is a sense in which a person's behavior forms the initial basis for an intelligence test score. In response to verbal acts by a tester, a subject utters sounds or moves objects around. Then, however, the acts by the subject are evaluated by the tester, points are assigned on the basis of evaluations, and, finally, all the points assigned are added up. There may or may not be further computations involved. When all this is done, can the result be called behavioral? Is the test score objective? If the answer to the first question is no, and the answer to the second question is yes, then behavior forms only a part of whatever it is that can be objectively measured about a person. The nonbehavioral part would start with behavior but would include evaluation of the behavior and interpretation of it as reflecting a characteristic that was not behavior. The objectivity of the resulting measure would be derived largely from the standardization of the evaluation process.

It is probably true that most people would regard the final intelligence score, or perhaps some of the subscores, as more important than the uninterpreted sounds and movements with which the evaluation process began.

Does behavior, then, refer to what people do overtly, explicitly, without any interpretation of what the behavior might mean, or does behavior refer to some combined package of overt acts and interpretations thereof? It is difficult to imagine how one might describe behavior without interpreting it. Simple assumptions about goal orientation are implicit even in such bare assertions as "depresses lever" or "responds to question." If some way could be found to describe human behavior intelligibly with no interpretation whatsoever, it seems likely that few people would be interested in it. It would be, almost by definition, meaningless.

As some interpretation is placed upon behavior, it begins to become interesting. A rash person might suggest that it is usually the interpretation that is interesting, and not the behavior at all, except as the behavior helps to make the interpretation more or less clear and/or more or less plausible.

Whether it is the uninterpreted physical activity or the interpretation that is the primary source of interest, it is usually the interpretation that makes the behavior interesting. It appears that some degree of interpretation must be included in a useful definition of behavior, but that beyond a certain point, the amount of interpretative processing—even though it may be objective—yields something that might not be thought of as behavior. An IQ may be derived from behavior but may not itself be regarded as a piece of behavior.

There are thus three points being made. The first of these is that it is possible to define behavior in such a way that objectivity is a broader concept than behavior. The score yielded by some test, for example, may be objective and may or may not be behavior, depending on how much interpretation, or other processing, is allowed before something stops being called behavior. The second point is that totally uninterpreted (or uninterpretable) human behavior is of relatively little interest. Almost everyone is interested in interpretation of behavior to one extent or another. It is the desired "amount" of interpretation that seems to vary so among observers. The third point follows from the second. It is that the resulting definition of behavior is not itself objective. The amount of (even standardized) interpretative processing allowed before derived entities are not regarded as behavior is not itself easy to specify in any objective way.

All of this leads to a fairly mundane definition of behavior as referring to packages of observable physical activity and some relatively low amount of interpretation of that activity. Activity with absolutely no interpretation is not very interesting. Activity with interpretation may be interesting. What about interpretation apart from any particular activity?

Let us continue to suppose that an interpretation process is so standardized that it will be regarded generally as objective. One question that remains is, why has some particular standardization process been selected? For example, the particular scoring assigned to intelligence test items only makes sense in the context of an interest in some particular set of inner states (lumped together under the heading of intelligence, or, perhaps, past learning). These states may be thought of as potentials for behavior, but there can be no doubt that a potential is not itself a behavior.

Perhaps this is only a semantic matter. If intelligence as a noun is turned into intelligent, an adjective, does any reference to inner states become unnecessary? The primary focus of concern can be intelligent behavior in and of itself. Two questions unmask this as only a semantic skirting of interests in things other than behavior. First, what is intelligent behavior? It will not do simply to point at examples. This would just be an item-oriented version of "intelligence is what intelligence tests measure." It might be difficult, although not necessarily impossible, to define what is intelligent about intelligent behavior without reference to such things as knowledge, thought, evidence of (invisible) logical operations, and memory. Second, and more decisive, is stability over time of concern? If so, then there is a propensity imagined (correctly or otherwise) that is generally present but only demonstrated visibly in selected situations. The study of intelligent behavior is quite likely to be based on a fundamental interest in this propensity, which is invisible, which is not behavior, and which is usually referred to by a noun—intelligence.

No amount of standardization, or assertion that intelligence is what intelligence tests measure, explains the way test items are oriented to ability or knowledge. Objectively tested or not, alleged inner states (ability or knowledge or potentials of various kinds), perhaps gussied up as hypothetical constructs, are likely to be the primary focus of interest. It seems likely that most professionals do not think of intelligence as hypothetical, but regard it, perhaps naively, as a real entity or as a collection of real entities. Furthermore, the particularities of behavior used to achieve inferences about these particular inner states are of relatively less importance than the states themselves.

If two tests are available that are highly correlated, but that use totally different items, investigators seem quite free to select one or the other on a variety of grounds, even including convenience. It is results that count most, and it seems to be believed that different behaviors can be used to achieve similar results.

What has been said about intelligence tests applies to any number of other procedures. There can be objectivity in the sense that most observers will agree on the score a person should be assigned along with a primary interest in an inference about one or more internal states, not behavior.

A test may not depend primarily on any particular behavior (since different behavioral items might be thought interchangeable) and yet still be regarded as fundamentally based on behavior; but this may require having history start somewhere in the middle of test construction. Since the constructed test is objective and is based on particular items of behavior, it can be said that the procedure is basically behavioral. But this conclusion is only available by turning away from the fact that test items were probably created because they seemed to point to some thing or things not behavioral in any direct or concrete sense whatsoever. In effect, the test is likely to be fundamentally based on (nonobjective) ideas about some alleged entity or entities that is or are not behavioral. The initial primary interest was not in behavior.

It would not be difficult to generate many examples in which the interpretation of behavior seems to be a more primary interest than the behavior itself, even without referring to clinical interests. However, there are also instances available in which behaviors themselves (including modest interpretation) seem to be a primary interest. These behaviors appear to fall into two general categories: extreme behaviors that have serious consequences no matter how they are viewed and behaviors that have acquired interest because of an historical connection to something else and have since taken on, as it were, a life of their own.

Examples of behavior in the first category might include such disasters as a person hitting another person hard enough to cause pain or injury, or someone driving a moving car into someone else. One positive example would be if someone would (please) give me a great deal of money with no legal strings attached. If getting married can be thought of as behavioral, it is something with certain consequences that apply across a wide range of possible interpretations. If war can be regarded as behavioral, it too can have consequences that may not depend heavily on how the war making is viewed.

In recent times, war may be fought for goals that are not behavioral, as in the idea of WHAM (winning hearts and minds). Similarly, the purposes or explanations for other behaviors in this category may or may not be viewed in behavioral terms, but the behaviors themselves remain a central interest because of their consequences.

Although the behaviors in this category may be *a* central interest, they are not *the* central interest. The most central interest is clearly in the consequences of these behaviors. The behaviors, apart from any interest due to interpretations, derive interest because of their connection to later events. Interest in these behaviors, as uninterpreted events, would diminish abruptly if they ceased to have important consequences.

The second category of behaviors of interest in and of themselves is a matter of some concern. Suppose a test is constructed more or less in the manner described earlier. Once constructed, the subjective origins of the test become only an inconvenience or an embarrassment. The objective test itself, divorced from the nonobjective ideas that led to its birth, becomes a primary object of interest after some evidence is collected that is thought to argue for its validity. An interest in the test is then regarded as basically a behavioral interest, since interest is thought to be primarily in the behaviors enacted in response to the test items.

Thus, an interest in objectivity leads to interests that are relatively removed from the people that variables are presumed to characterize. One comes to study tests and variables instead of people. Perhaps this progression does not often happen; but if it does, and if it happens because of a concern for objectivity, one might wonder whether the concern for objectivity has gone too far.

Most human behavior that does not fall into these two categories seems to be interesting to other humans primarily because of what it signifies and/or because of its alleged (or real) connection to some internal state or states. Some apparent interest in behavior per se may seem otherwise if considered closely.

At first glance, sexual behavior might seem to be an ultimate example of behavior that is intrinsically interesting. It is a clinical commonplace, however, that people gain or (more often) lose sexual interest abruptly when situations change, for example, when a lover turns into a spouse or when the other person's attitude becomes seen as demeaning. Few adults may be consistently interested exclusively in sexual behavior without regard to what it means about the people around them or about themselves. Even masturbation seems to be as much a fantasy trip as a physical one.

If all the conditional vicissitudes of sexual interest are disregarded (after all, would I have thought interest to be so conditional when I was 15?), the primary basis for the personal interest that most people have is still not some behavioral act itself. Clearly, the primary interest is due to the connection between overt acts and an internal state, namely sexual feeling. Few people find behavioral descriptions of orgasm to be as interesting as the subjective experience. It is in fact complaints about subjective experience that have led to an interest in studying orgastic behavior. One of the most notable features of human sexuality is that the physical acts involved are quite varied. What they have most in common is that they excite lust. When acts that usually seem sexual fail to excite lust, interest visibly wanes.

Even learning theorists do not seem to be particularly interested in behaviors as such. In a sense, they may care less than most other people since they may care little about differences among different kinds of behavior. For some purposes, one behavior may be thought as good as another. Behaviors may be selected for scrutiny primarily on the basis of one kind of convenience or other. What is more of interest, apparently, is some alleged internal state (learning) and/or some set of relationships among behaviors and other events. If learning is regarded as an internal state, the primary interest of learning theorists is certainly an internal state. If not, the primary interest is still not any given behavior. Probably few people really care about bar pressing per se. The primary interest is in something that hangs in the air, as it were, among the observed events. It is in the organization of events, not in the events themselves.

Apart from connotations, some ideas about internal states may be only marginally different from ideas about the organization of external events. "Internal" does not imply that a geographical location is known as much as it implies that what is perceived directly leads people to believe in the existence of other things that are not perceived directly, some of which may be logically "behind" what is perceived. We perceive our own phenomenological worlds, and hence believe that other people do so also. Expressions of such things as knowledge lead us to believe that potentials for these expressions exist and are carried around invisibly. The organization of complex external activity in general seems difficult to characterize, much less explain, without reference to organizing factors that might not be directly observable. There may be a fine line, if any line at all, between asserting the existence of organization, and asserting the existence of organizing factors.

While discussing the meaning of "internal states," it should be noted also that "internal" need not imply a focus on an individual person. Except perhaps for phenomenology, the question of whether dyads and

larger groups can be regarded in analogous ways might well be a matter
to be judged on the basis of results.

This chapter so far has focused more on behavior than on objectivity.
Among other things, it has suggested that objectivity is a broader
concept than behavior, and that the definition of behavior is not itself a
totally objective matter. More important, it has been argued that most
people—either in their roles as ordinary citizens or as professionals in
social science or therapy—are less interested in behavior than one might
think at first glance. Most of us, in spite of some possible protestations
to the contrary, seem to be interested primarily in other things. Behavior
becomes interesting largely because of its real or alleged connection to
internal states, to other interesting interpretations, or to consequences.
Sometimes, although no particular behavior is very interesting, there is
interest in the organization of behavior and other events. In short,
behavior itself is not exceptionally interesting stuff.

Perhaps these views are overstated. If so, it may be that some
overstatement is appropriate. The view that behavior is "obviously" of
primary importance needs to be confronted with the fact than an
opposite view is possible and perhaps even plausible.

It seems to be widely believed that insight is unrelated to behavior
change. Presumably this belief implies that something other than
behavior can be measured, since it is implicit that insight can be
evaluated and that it is not behavior. This belief is usually asserted by
way of arguing that insight has little value. My own view should be clear
from all that has been said so far. It is that this belief, if it is true, is an
argument against the importance of behavior change.

There may be a trick in this last argument. After all, clients exist who
will say that they desperately want to stop doing X, and that knowing X
to be a consequence or an expression of such and such is not helping
them stop doing it. This is not the place to belabor the likelihood that
what such clients report is something other than insight. The more
pertinent observation is that X is very likely to be a package of behavior
and interpretation involving quite substantial interpretation on the
client's part. That is, X is likely to be important because it means
something important to the client, something to do with self-worth, for
example. Assuming a therapist with magical power to change one or the
other but not both, would it be more important to change the behavior
or the client's view of her or his behavior? Changing the behavior might
be justified on the basis of a belief that one result will be a change in the

client's inner state. Changing the client's inner state—in this case an interpretation of behavior—requires no such justification.

What about behaviors with serious consequences? Is there not a justification for changing them regardless of any client view of them? Perhaps, unless the consequences are not really inevitable. First, the question should be raised of how far afield we want to go. Some examples of such behavior have more to do with socialization or even law enforcement than socially oriented therapy. Second, consequences are not always inevitable and may depend on things more subtle than crass behavior. If the consequences can be changed without the behavior changing, why worry about the behavior?

This last suggestion seems a little strange and far fetched, so let us back off from it for a bit and consider two clinical anecdotes.

> Jones is a therapeutic client who has little income under her personal control, although her husband's income is substantial. The therapist expresses curiosity that she has embarked on a therapeutic enterprise with very little apparent ability to pay for it. The next time Jones appears, she announces that after a confrontation with her husband, he has agreed to subsidize her therapy.

> Smith is a therapeutic client who has little income under her personal control, although her husband's income is substantial. The therapist expresses curiosity that she has embarked on a therapeutic enterprise with very little apparent ability to pay for it. The next time Smith appears, she announces that after some thought she has decided that the therapist is right. She is going to quit therapy.

There is nothing particularly exciting about the thought that the same behavior addressed to two different people may have different consequences. Let us assume, therefore, that differences between Smith and Jones are not the main reason for this different result. What else could explain such a different result if the therapist enacted the same behaviors in both cases?

Backing off still further, notice that behavior has been implicitly regarded as objective and that objectivity has been characterized in terms of close agreement among observers, judges, or test scorers. There is thus a joker hidden in this definition of behavior. It is that an objective behavior is a package of activity and (low-level) interpretation that is defined concretely enough so that there is little ambiguity about its recognition by an available scoring device (probably, but not necessarily, a human device). The frailty of social science in its observational abilities is thus built into this definition by necessity. If behavior can be recognized only ambiguously, it is not objective. Considering that observer agreement is not exactly facilitated by requiring subtlety of judgment, objective behavior is perforce relatively crass behavior.

Therefore there are two ways the therapist could enact the same behaviors and have very different consequences. One is that the actions are different in subtleties that are not objective—they are beyond the limits of an objective observational system. The other is that the same behaviors are enacted but are orchestrated in subtly different ways that escape an objective observational system. The timing or sequencing may be different, or the acts themselves may be different, in such a way as to lead to a different result with the client but not with an available objective observational system.

The crassness of objective behavior is not just an incidental feature that can be disregarded when convenient. Potential objectivity is central to a concern with behavior. The fact is that there may be serious limits to objectivity and that those limits might not include subtleties of some importance.

If one thinks in terms of intentions, it is possible that the therapist had different intentions with Jones than with Smith and that these different intentions led to the same set of behaviors (defined as above) having different consequences. If so, an observer not quite so oriented to concrete objectivity just might pick up differences in intention without being at all clear about specific differences in behavior. If pressed, such an observer might say that the intentions did not show in any particular action but were apparent in slight stylistic things that were difficult to pin down and/or were somehow in the air between actions—that is, they showed in the organization of actions.

It might be objected that, in effect, clients are assumed to perceive aspects of performance that are missed by professional observers. This is absolutely true, if it is clear that the professional observation in question is observation of concrete, objective behaviors. In effect, such an observer may be looking only at trees or even only at large trees. A client, under no such restraints, may have a much more clear view of the woods. There are also two other related points. The first is that a client may have some substantial history of past conversations and therefore be able to pick up slight changes in what is going on more readily than the professional observer. The second is that the existence of different reactions by the two clients does not necessarily imply anything at all about the clients' awareness or their ability to report the basis for differences.

This kind of thing happens all around us. One person uses corporal punishment with his or her children, and so does another. Yet in one case there seem to be serious consequences, and there seem to be no visible consequences whatever in the other. It may be that the difference is directly demonstrable to be a crass instance of different timing—that is, a grossly different reinforcement pattern. It is possible, however, that nothing so simple can actually be demonstrated and that there are large differences in how apparently similar behavior is interpreted in the two situations.

One person tells jokes at the expense of the boss and is fired. Another does the same thing and is promoted. If behavior is to be used only to refer to something that can be described objectively, which is to say crassly, there are likely to be any number of ways in which people can change without their behavior changing but with meaningful changes in the consequences of that behavior. Since it can be assumed that couples and families are more complex behaviorally than individuals, the opportunities they provide for subtle variations in behavior and in the organization of behavior are likely to be even greater.

Starting with a loose definition of behavior that seemed to encompass almost everything, we have moved to a much more restrictive definition and to suggestions about other classifications for phenomena of interest. There is behavior in the narrow sense described above. There is objective information about people, which includes but is not limited to objective behavior. There are meanings or alleged inner states of one kind or another that, it has been urged, are usually more interesting than behavior per se. There are subtleties in behavior that might be real without being objectively (unambiguously) observable. Finally, there is the organization of what people do, which might have features crass enough to be captured objectively, but which is likely also to have subtleties that escape an objective observational system.

Inner states, by definition, cannot be known directly except for some of our own. To speak of someone else's feelings, intentions, abilities, or attitudes means to make inferences based on externals. It might be argued that since everything external is behavior, reference to another person's inner states is really only a reference to selected aspects of behavior that are referred to, mistakenly, as inner states. At best, inner states (perhaps except our own) are hypothetical constructs not to be confused with real entities.

First, such a statement requires that the definition of behavior be extended to include nuances that cannot be objectified, to include the organization of behavior (both subtle and not so subtle), to include demonstrable (but invisible) potentials for behavior, and to include information that may result from extensive processing of behavior (processing that may make no sense unless some ideas about inner states exist as givens). Jones may make an inference about what her husband's behavior means because she has lived with him for 20 years. Are we to regard even the outcome of this processing as a report of her husband's behavior? To say that everything we know about each other depends on behavior requires so loose a definition of behavior that it loses a claim to being objective or objectifiable.

Still, whether a restrictive definition of behavior is used, or a definition is employed that includes everything external plus any amount of processing, is it not true that inner states of other people cannot be known directly and that inferences about inner states are really just speculatively loaded descriptions of externals? Is it not true that inner states are only hypothetical constructs?

To say that something is "just" or "only" something else is to suggest that it is unimportant, without actually saying so. On the contrary, inner states may be quite important. If so, it is not crucial whether inner states are regarded as explanatory fictions, as possibilities, or as logical necessities. Personally, I believe (itself an assertion of an inner state) that some inner states, or so-called explanatory fictions, actually exist and that most of my colleagues feel (another such assertion) the same way. With or without this belief, most of us find it convenient, or helpful, or interesting, to act as if these entities are real. Having taken that stand, we—or most of us—may find that it is these entities in which we take a primary interest.

No one actually sees subatomic particles. Evidence about their existence is based on other things that can be observed more directly, plus a complex set of inferential assumptions. Yet some people are convinced that they study subatomic particles and might take umbrage at the thought that what they really study is the laboratory equipment that constitutes all they can see directly. If it is to be said that all we "really" study is externals, the next step or two might as well be taken leading to the conclusion that for many social scientists, social science is the study of computer printouts.

As Kuhn (1970) suggested, science (what he referred to as "normal" science) involves taking a stand on some view of reality, acting as if that view is what reality really is, and then interpreting evidence in the light of that view. If a stand is taken that includes allegations about reality that transcend mere externals, it may or may not be fruitful. There is no a priori reason for ruling it out or regarding it as less "real" than some other stand. Since most people, including most professionals in our fields, seem implicitly to take one version or another of such a stand, it seems foolish and erroneous to regard it as less scientific than a study of externals. It seems almost perverse to regard crass studies of peripheral phenomena as somehow more central than consideration of what might be at the heart of things.

9

FREEDOM FROM VALUES

In 1963 Alfred Hitchcock made a film called *The Birds*. It was about a rural area in which the local birds went berzerk for unexplained reasons and did violence to property and people. Some viewers might have found this film frightening. Bosley Crowther, then reviewing films for the *New York Times*, said it was the best comedy of the year. It seemed then that Crowther was not exactly being sarcastic or that he thought the film to be unintentionally funny. To understand what he was saying, it was helpful to understand something about where Crowther was, in more recent terminology, "coming from." Given a critic's judgment, and given an idea of the critic's values and worldview, in a sense, it is possible to perform a sort of triangulation. One can then estimate roughly what it is the critic is describing as understood from one's own point of view. In the case at hand, Crowther might have meant that Hitchcock's attitude of amused cynicism toward his audience, toward his own film, and maybe toward life in general was amply displayed in *The Birds*. For example, the film builds up to a dramatic climax that never happens. Hitchcock just walks away from it at the end and leaves the filmgoer dangling.

Professional critics make a good contrast to social scientists (therapists are a more mixed bag), since critics pass judgments for a living, and social scientists who own up to value judgments in their professional work are relatively rare. I wonder which group is relied on more by the average citizen.

The task of social science is to characterize what is, not to pass judgment upon it. Is this not so? Therapists must judge some things to be better than others, since they help people change, but even they are "supposed" to be nonjudgmental in some respects and to see things as they are, not as one might wish them to be. Is and ought are different. The business of social science, and to some extent the business of therapy, is the former term and not the latter.

It is true that a preoccupation with nonjudgmental factuality has led to some statements that seem almost bizarre because they omit value judgment. For example, dry recitations of how many people are to be killed outright, or die a more agonizing death, or be hideously wounded, in case of "nuclear attack" sound almost as if they come from machines rather than from people. Roszak (1972), in his critique of science in general, quotes Blake to suggest that scientists see the world "through dead men's eyes."

Still, the burden of this essay is not to pass judgment on the intention to be nonjudgmental. It is more to ask how well this intention can possibly succeed, and whether an excess of this intention can produce opposite effects to those desired. Perhaps the goal of a relatively value-free discipline would be better served by easing off a little on the determination to appear value free. Perhaps, in other words, values might be easier to deal with if they came out of hiding.

It gets cumbersome to refer repeatedly to "nonjudgmental" or "value free." For the purposes of this essay, "descriptive" will be used to refer to characterizations of reality that are free of value judgment. No implication of objectivity is intended in any sense other than that the characterizations are nonjudgmental. Objective or not, no necessary implication of validity is intended by this term. One question then is whether purely descriptive characterizations of people actually exist.

Perhaps an observer's values make up a point of view in the sense that they are essential for seeing and for characterizing the world. Since it is not possible to describe something from no point of view, it is not possible to describe something without taking one judgmental stand or another.

This argument is not very persuasive. It seems unlikely that all aspects of an observer's point of view will be pertinent for each and every observation. In particular, it is easy to imagine ways in which personal values are irrelevant.

Parents of a newborn have a strong investment in the child having the usual number of fingers and toes, but this fact is logically irrelevant to the actual counts. If it affects the counts a parent makes, it does so not as a matter of point of view but as a distorting bias. This is very different from parents wanting their child to grow up to be a successful human being. Success is partly a value judgment itself and therefore is a term that cannot be understood without knowing the value stance of those making it. Parental values are not a distorting influence in this second case. On the contrary, if the parents should claim to be value free when they express this wish, one would doubt them, and/or one might wonder what they meant.

By my count, there are three major ways in which values enter into observational work and therefore become pertinent (omitting values as a basis for choosing directions in which a therapist might support change). The first is that values, as interests, affect what is observed. In the example above, parents take an intense and very personal interest in getting accurate and value-free information about their newborn child. Similarly, one might be intensely interested in the success of some political cause and therefore be determined to do absolutely unbiased research in the service of selecting the best possible campaign strategy.

The second major way that values enter into observational work is by introducing direct bias. There is a sense in which results can be thought factually—that is, descriptively—wrong because perception or report has been shifted by observers' values. Jules Henry (1965) took a dim view of what went on in the households of schizophrenics. Since he "knew" beforehand that these homes had bred disasters, it is possible that his descriptions were colored—biased—by his prejudices.

The third route that values take is distinguished from the second in that it might not lead to assertions that are actually wrong. Instead, there is a kind of value encryption and by the same token an encryption of descriptive material. Description and evaluation are welded together, perhaps even in individual words, in ways that may be difficult or impossible to decode.

The concept of success is a clear example of value (and descriptive fact) encryption. If one knows the evaluative point of view in use, it is possible to determine what is asserted descriptively. If one knows appropriate descriptive facts, it might be possible to figure out the standards of value in use. If neither of these conditions is satisfied, "success" is a cryptic assertion with an undecodable meaning.

Suppose Smith is called intelligent, without further explanation. Most likely, Smith has been both described and complimented. It might be impossible to determine the extent to which intelligence refers to descriptive characteristics of Smith and the extent to which it refers to the observer's—or to a consensual—positive evaluation of these characteristics. If values of the observer—or of all of us—are hidden in this term (intelligence) that purports to be descriptive, it can be said that value encryption has occurred. The values actually may be buried in the definition of intelligence, or some other term, in which case no error has been made. The definition of the term, value judgment and all, has been followed.

The impact of values impinging on observational work is affected by their visibility. For example, although it is obvious that one's interests affect the direction of one's attentions as a generality, it may not be so clear in some individual case. An author may say that a problem is pursued because of scientific necessity or because of some other agent that is outside the pursuer. It is doubtful that social science is developed anywhere to the extent that "scientific necessity" can be defined, but that is not the point. The point is that if one's personal interests have led in a particular direction, but scientific respectability has demanded that some other rationale be provided to justify the direction, an invitation has been provided to make things up.

It would be possible at this point to argue that rationales provided under such circumstances are misleading and lead to expensive consequences, but that would be an example of something like the thing being criticized. The fact is that probably few people are seriously misled by these gestures toward scientific respectability. It seems likely that people usually just skim over them and go on to more important aspects of content. Perhaps my objection is only a matter of taste: It would be nicer if people were permitted to skip pretentious and possibly exaggerated justifications for their work and to get on with the work itself.

This is not a suggestion, by the way, that no work is done for reasons that flow logically from other work, nor that no work is important. It is only a suggestion that "mere" interest ought to be enough to justify a piece of work. "Mere" interest will be the actual reason for much work being done anyway, whether overtly or not.

Bias, of course, is something else. Since bias is not always easy to discern, some clear idea of an observer's values may help in its discovery, or in an argument that bias is unlikely, or in correcting for bias by taking an appropriate measure of salt.

What is most perplexing about bias is that bias implies error, and error implies that definable truth exists. Thus, the point of view of the observer, or of an observer of the observer, is important in two ways: in defining values that might or might not distort descriptions and in defining a stand taken about reality.

One standard tactic for minimizing the effects of bias is to use observers who are "blind" to some important fact. If codings are to be made of letters written by schizophrenics and by neurotics, coders may be kept blind about which letters were written by which classification of person. Sometimes, as in a test comparing two medications, subjects themselves may be kept blind about which experimental treatment they receive. No subject knows which medication has been administered, and no judge of improvement knows it either, so any differences that emerge between treatment groups are attributable to real differences in the medications. At least that is the way this double-blind procedure is supposed to work.

As indicated in the essay on contextuality, such a procedure only prevents an observer from being formally told which subject is in which group. In spite of everyone's best efforts, a subject may drop some relatively trivial clue that tells the observer anyway. Everything after that can then be affected by bias. Differences between descriptions of different groups remain *ultimately* attributable to real differences in what is observed, in the sense that they can be traced back to whatever it was that tipped off the observer. The differences in what was actually observed may not, however, be much like the differences in potentially biased observer reports.

Procedural arrangements such as the double blind are designed to prevent experimental groups from being differentiated on the basis of differential bias. To locate bias in any absolute sense means somehow to be able to specify what is real. This may seem easy when counting baby's fingers and toes, but there are situations in which it is not so easy and in which the distinction between reality and bias may be thought important.

Defining reality as consensus is begging the question. Suppose an international gymnastic event is judged by a group of persons from one country only. People suspect that these judges are biased but are unable to prove it. Suppose a second team of judges is brought in from another country, and differences between the two sets of judges are manifest and substantial. This may be thought to prove differences in bias, but it says nothing about which team of judges is biased or whether they both are. If judges are brought in from all over the world, is the average of their views a measure of reality, or only a measure of average bias? Perhaps averaging over all judges will provide only an indirect measure of world politics as each judge favors the athletes with a like ideology.

Is it vacuous to worry about a distinction between consensus and reality? In my opinion, it may not be vacuous except in the special case where consensus refers not to an average but to the fact that there is virtually total agreement on a matter.

Suppose that in the case of this athletic event, a representative of each team of judges sits down with you and goes over a film of the competition. Each judge makes clear to you exactly what he or she has responded to in each and every evaluation of gymnastic performance. Assuming you have the interest and energy to sit through this experience and pay attention, by the time it is over, you will likely have some clear idea of where each team of judges is "coming from." You might develop some conviction about "actual" reality, a position that might not be some simple average. It might be, in fact, a position that *transcends* the different points of view you have heard. That is, you might develop your own (meta) point of view of the different realities that exist according to the orientations of the differing teams of judges. Finally, you might acquire a less simple idea of bias and become able to speak of a team of judges making decisions that are wrong even according to their own explicated standards.

Infinite regress is inescapable. It is clear that there is no view of reality that cannot be transcended by a still more encompassing view that shows it to be conditional. To pursue the gymnastic example, a first level of description is that one athletic performance is judged to be of higher quality than another. After some investigation, an observer of differences among judges might have some view of what is "really" going on. She or he might say that one team of judges emphasizes grace and smoothness, whereas another puts relatively greater emphasis on demonstrated physical strength and sureness. The next logical level would mean investigating differences among observers of the judges. One very well might find that different observers find different ways to characterize differences among judges. A meta-observer might even assert that while one observer attributes differences among judges to one set of things, and another observer attributes them to another set of things, what is "really" going on that is being characterized in these several ways is . . . and so on.

There is a difference between merely accepting an average as defining reality and seeking to understand differences among, say, judges, and to locate them within a more comprehensive view. The former process drops a problem by declaring it vacuous. The latter one seeks to understand a problem and involves (1) acquiring information about judge's values, (2) gathering information about differing views of reality, and (3) taking some more encompassing view that can make sense of diverse judgments. Alleging that observers have no values, or keeping them hidden, obstructs this latter curiosity while providing few obvious benefits.

Seeking to understand differences among judges can seem like a kind of preoccupation with rarified abstractions as the brute facts of the original judgments are delicately teased apart. The fact is that this seeking to understand requires getting a lot closer to the raw material being studied than does an averaging of diverse numbers.

Judgments of reality sometimes seem a lot easier than this. We look at something, and there it is, both real and obvious. If we believe that someone's count of a child's fingers or toes is really accurate, is it because we can see the reality directly for ourselves, or is it because we have learned that there is a great deal of consensus on counts of this sort? Alternatively, is there a great deal of consensus because each of us can see the reality directly? What does "directly" mean?

Harry Stack Sullivan may be as responsible as anyone for some confusion, at least in clinical circles, between consensus and reality. Although Sullivan's thinking (1953) therefore has had some influence, it was also fairly idiosyncratic. Perhaps this fact itself suggests that more attention needs to be paid to the distinction between consensus and reality.

Consensus has the advantage of not requiring an individual to take a stand that such and such is what is real, even if a democratic process suggests otherwise. The price, however, can be considerable. On the Rorschach test, a most unusual response might be thought out of touch with reality just because it is unusual, or it might be thought exceptionally perceptive and creative because the tester can see the response clearly once the subject has pointed it out. There is a difference.

There is also, of course, a price attached to taking a stand about what is real. It is that this is one more way that the observer, and the observer's point of view, cannot readily be subtracted from what is observed. In the Rorschach example, it might be just too bad for a testee if the testee is original, creative, and perceptive, and the tester is none of these.

Was Picasso lucky to have grown up in a society where children who were different did not get a psychological assessment?

If absolute consensus exists, in the sense that virtually all observers agree almost totally, the distinction between consensual validity and "real" validity disappears from sight. That is, if everyone sees things the same way, the distinction between consensus and reality becomes quite invisible.

Wilcox (1964) has argued that absolute consensus is a way to cross the imaginary bridge between is and ought. If everyone (at all times) agrees on a certain value, we might as well concede that we ought to support it. In response, (1) this is an option not likely to be taken consciously, since in the situation described, the distinction between is and ought is likely to be unnoticed, and (2) "all times" can never mean more than "all past times." There will be some elaboration in a while on the fact that the future can bring surprises.

To summarize, discovering bias, correcting for it, and understanding it are likely to be facilitated by and in some cases may actually require several things. These include knowing something about the values of observers suspected of bias, knowing something about their views of reality, and taking some more encompassing view of reality oneself. It is likely that bias cannot be ruled out absolutely in many situations. If so, one essential task of a research consumer, for example, must be an attempt to understand the nature of potential bias, and correct for it. This attempt is not helped if those who write reports are obliged to present themselves as impartial, or if the judges used in an observational task are thought to have no values. Paradoxically, if some degree of bias were more acceptable, it might be easier to learn the sorts of things that would help one take it into account and hence reduce its impact.

Value encryption is perhaps the most subtle of the ways that values enter into descriptive work, although it can be crass on occasion. The idea of a successful marriage is an example of a concept that seems to have been pursued by a great deal of allegedly descriptive (that is, nonevaluative) work, over a substantial period of time. Clearly, marriage success is not a purely descriptive term. It describes an alleged relationship between what is (in some couple's marriage) and what (in the view of a person using this concept) ought to be. To decode marriage success—that is, to determine what is—one must first acquire a descriptive definition of what ought to be. Since there is likely to be less than total agreement among social scientists or therapists concerning such a descriptive definition, assertions of marriage success do not actually describe, and may be impossible to "factor," as it were, into a portion that is descriptive and a portion that is evaluative.

Let us take a close look at the concept of marriage success and some similar terms. We can pass over blatant circularity, as in a suggestion that a successful marriage is a good marriage. But what about happiness? If everyone agrees that happiness is the definition of success in marriage, everyone will understand what marriage success means, and it becomes (as good as) a purely descriptive term. The trouble is, of course, that "happiness" may be itself a term in which value encryption has occurred. Suppose a couple maintains a cheery disposition by doing things that are much disvalued, such as kicking the children around, or by taking heroin injections. Perhaps such a couple would find itself accused of not being "really" happy, or alternatively not being "really" successful. An easy way out, apparently, is to define success according to what the couple wants, but that would depend as much on general agreement as any other value judgment. Would everyone agree that a successful marriage means one that satisfies a couple's standards? What about couples with low standards? What about the couple whose standards include things most people find abhorrent, such as child abuse, spouse abuse, or incest?

Marriage satisfaction, like happiness, seems at first glance to describe an alleged internal state (satisfaction) and not to pass judgment on it. The most used questionnaire measure of marriage satisfaction (Locke & Wallace, 1959) suggests otherwise. Along with some questions that ask more directly about satisfaction, spouses are asked to report such things as being "on the go" and disagreements. They are not asked how much they are satisfied by these things.

There are a variety of terms that have been used in place of "success" over the years. Marriage satisfaction is the most popular and the latest seems to be marital quality. The idea of "distress" has also been employed, as in distinctions between distressed and nondistressed couples. All of these terms refer in one way or another to distinctions between preferred or good marriages and less preferred or bad marriages. Each of these terms, as usually employed, probably includes some value encryption and hence does not refer exclusively to descriptive facts. This guess is bolstered by the fact that they are consistently preferred over such less ambiguously descriptive terms such as "marital complaints" or "marriage duration."

Some terms involve value encryption in ways that may be far from obvious. "Ability," for example, seems at first glance, to be a word that does not have value judgment hidden within it. Yet, other things being equal, ability implies a higher evaluation than the absence of ability.

I was once the moderator of a debate between two well-known people in the family field, the subject of the debate being extramarital sex. One participant took a positive view of spouses being sexually active with outsiders. He agreed amiably that not everyone had the ability to deal with this sort of thing, but thought that it might be worthwhile for those who could handle it. The other person supported monogamous sexuality. He took a sympathetic attitude toward those people who were not able to content themselves with monogamy but thought monogamy was probably a good thing for those with the ability to manage it.

It is certainly possible that descriptive entities can be liked or disliked without values being hidden in the definitions of the entities. If enough people prefer Cadillacs to Chevrolets, the terms will acquire connotations that are differentially value laden. However, the definition of Cadillac, or of Chevrolet, does not include value judgment. It is possible, without violating a definition, to prefer a Chevrolet to a Cadillac. Is it possible to think stupidity is more worthwhile than intelligence, as a general rule, without violating customary definitions?

There may be any number of clues as to the existence of value encryption. For instance, agreement in value tone between alleged cause and effect, as discussed in an earlier essay, may be one such clue. An actual demonstration of value encryption depends on what happens to an apparently descriptive fact when it is seen through the eyes of people with different values.

Suppose it is said that spouses from the same ethnic group have more successful marriages than spouses from different ethnic groups. The evidence used is drawn from divorce statistics, which show that the latter kinds of marriages are more likely to end in divorce. Now, imagine a person who does not believe in long marriages. From this person's point of view, marriage is like going to college. The goal is to graduate, not to stay there forever. Furthermore, the better persons graduate sooner. From the point of view of this mythical person, the conclusion described above would be factually incorrect. If such a strange point of view is a little too much, what about an attitude that something in the kind of relationship between spouses is more important than simple endurance? Surely it is possible, regardless of divorce statistics, that there is something uniquely attractive about marriages between ethnic groups.

Imagine a demonstration that psychotherapy works. What would that mean? "Works" must refer to some descriptive change that is in the direction someone prefers. It will not do to say that change is in the direction of mental health, since it is difficult to imagine a term with more (poorly) hidden values than mental health. What is improvement to an observer with one set of values may be something else to an observer who values other things. The so-called criterion problem does not have an empirical solution, but requires putting in descriptive terms what it is one values. There is no way to guarantee that the value-free terms needed to do this even exist.

Many allegations that one thing is better than another might be accurate for people with one set of values and false for people whose values are very different. Examples are easy to provide: Sexual relationships are better with simultaneous mutual orgasms. Evidence proves that traditional marriages are better than egalitarian ones. Home care is better than institutional child care. Education emphasizing the three Rs is better than an emphasis on emotional development. If there has to be only one parent, children usually do better with their mothers than with their fathers. Unless "better" means better for some clearly descriptive purpose, it is a value-encrypted term.

Again, value encryption can be discovered by a confrontation with real or imaginary opposing values. To take another example from films, in Neil Simon's *Goodbye Girl* there is a scene in which a woman knocks on the door to a man's room and asks whether he is decent. Since he answers in the affirmative, she enters. He is, of course, naked.

Perhaps there is some general consensus concerning a particular value. All persons agree, and seem always to have agreed, that such and such is the way things should be. If this is really true, it would probably be difficult to spot. If an alternative value is not even imagined, a value may be totally invisible. Perhaps there is not much point in worrying about invisible values except for the troubling possibility that they may not stay that way.

Diamonds, let us say, are found in rocky ground. A research report on the subject says simply that some "precious stones" are found in rocky ground, which would be true. Time passes. Suppose the time comes when diamonds are no longer so valuable. Perhaps their industrial uses have passed, their use for personal adornment has become very unfashionable, and no one really is interested in buying them. The statement referred to above has become factually false. It is no longer true that "precious stones" are found in the kind of place described. Only diamonds are found there. A person reading the original report might be misled, but only if the earlier evaluation of diamonds were unknown.

In other words, results based on invisibly value-encrypted terms might be written not on water, but on ice, as it were. When time passes, the ice may melt, and results that were once true are true no more.

In case the example above seems too preposterous, here is one that is not so clear-cut, but that is real. In 1963 Tharp reviewed empirical research on marriage. His conclusion from this empirical work came close to suggesting that the way to have a better marriage is to conform to traditional sex roles. Is it possible that differences between his conclusions and conclusions that might be drawn from the same work today might have something to do with unanticipated changes in consensual values within social science?

If we are to take seriously the goal of a relatively nonjudgmental social science, value encryption might need to be taken seriously. Supposedly descriptive terms that have values hidden in their definitions do not describe very well. If socially oriented therapy is not to pursue narrow ideological or other goals inadvertently, in the name of mental health, maturity, good coping, adequate functioning, or adaptive behavior, the implicit evaluation in such terms might deserve more attention.

A patient had been thrown out by her previous therapist because, after substantial treatment, she still did something that showed her to be extremely immature. Her crime? Participating in an antiwar demonstration. It is no doubt unusual for a person to be "diagnosed" on the basis of such an act, but this example is probably not unique.

Getting rid of values is both impossible and undesirable. A value-free researcher would do no research. A value-free therapist would be a ship without a rudder. On the other hand, what we do or observe should, according to my values, be explicit enough so that others can understand it and even recast it in some sensible way according to their own, differing, points of view. Some of us may be fine enough to avoid actual bias, in the sense described in this essay, but few of us if any are likely to avoid embedding our values in our work in one way or another. A later consumer may find it difficult to disentangle values and descriptive facts, or—worse—may fail to notice that the tangle exists. If our own values are kept secret, the task of disentangling values and descriptions may even be impossible.

More permission to ourselves and to each other to express our values clearly may have two consequences. One is the consequence emphasized above, that values cryptically contained in allegedly descriptive materials might more easily be dealt with. The other is that it might increase self-conscious awareness of values, and reduce the temptation to really believe that what we like or dislike are actually descriptive facts, like psychiatric diagnoses. Values being more explicit in our work might mean less in the way of values smuggled in under the guise of descriptive facts.

IV

CHANGING

10

MINIMAL THERAPY

Minimal therapy results from taking a particular set of stands and following the stands out to their apparent implications. These particular stands cannot claim to be uniquely correct, as there is nothing uniquely correct (by definition) about any given stand. Those who start from different positions, even positions that are similar but not exactly the same, will of course come to different conclusions.

Some aspects of the positions described here are clearly matters of value. Some might even be regarded as ethical values. The resulting dilemma is that this chapter will be expressing, even arguing for, particular values (and some implications that may seem extreme) at the same time that the chapter itself is an expression and example of the fact that it is possible to take many different positions, each of which would result in a consistent and sensible view of therapy. Partly for reasons of human frailty, and partly because of a fundamental aspect of what this book asserts, there is the danger of perceiving in this chapter the conviction that there is one and only one proper set of views and an implicit condemnation of those who differ.

The human frailty involved is the fairly trivial fact that I tend to get carried away with evangelical fervor and to argue by exaggeration. I am serious, certainly, but not deadly serious, and even I will disagree with myself, here and there and tomorrow. The more important point is the proposal made by this book as a whole that one must do two things at once. First, one should recognize that there are many alternative views available of any given situation, some of them mutually exclusive. Second, one should (and must) actually choose among the available alternatives, even if only temporarily. One adopts a particular set of views *as if* it were uniquely correct. The broad range of choices, once acknowledged, is set aside by the act of choosing. If choices are taken with genuine commitment, "as if" then becomes incorrect. The end result is an unfixable tension between genuinely accepting a broad range of choices and at the same time genuinely rejecting the choices not taken.

Thus this section is an exercise in applying some of what has been proposed in earlier chapters. Like some of the earlier chapters, this one has its metaphoric aspects as well. Suggesting how clients are or might be regarded might yield some thoughts about how we could regard each other, our research subject matter, our work in general. Let me not deceive you, however. Although this chapter may be an exercise, and although it may be an extended metaphor, it is also a statement of what I think about therapy.

Furthermore, the stands taken here, although not necessarily the implications drawn from them, may not be very different from stands taken by many other therapists, perhaps even by most other therapists.

There is nothing remarkable about an insight-oriented approach to psychotherapy (or marriage or family therapy). There is nothing novel about an emphasis on clients' responsibility for their own lives. I am hardly alone in disclaiming deliberate deception and manipulation. Carl Whitaker has already expressed the view that technique is what one does while waiting for the therapist to arrive. Minimal therapy puts these things together in one package with some self-conscious effort at a clear value orientation and an intelligible epistemology. Perhaps this exercise will provide some slightly different ways of understanding what a therapist might do, to a therapist's (and hence to a client's) advantage. One intended suggestion will be that an excessive interest in changing other people, dramatically, rapidly, with whatever "things to do" are at hand, can have costs that outweigh the benefits.

Minimal therapy is mostly defined by what the therapist tries not to do because of stands taken about what is real and what is important. It is therapy, in effect, with one hand tied behind one's back. From a behavioral point of view, minimal therapy is very poorly defined, since it is relatively unconcerned with concrete, overt actions by either therapist or client. The greater concern is with their intentions.

Minimal therapy is not likely to appeal to beginners who want concrete things to do. It is not likely to appeal to therapists facing situations so desparate that they justify any action whatsoever. After all, no one would want an adolescent to starve to death, a child to be beaten silly, an older person to have a heart attack, or a homicide committed in order to preserve some civilized nicety of the therapeutic relationship. It is not likely to appeal to those who look for rapid and relatively easy ways to induce change, perhaps in response to long waiting lists and short resources.

Rejoinders are available for some of these hypothetical groups of people. The beginner doing concrete things may begin to feel after a while that something is missing. Perhaps that something has to do with a human quality that is left out of a relationship when people throw techniques at each other. Of course people must do structured things when they feel that the alternative is to drown, but they need not freeze their development at that level. They need not regard temporary necessity as an ideal situation.

Similarly, some catastrophes are so urgent and so terrible that all other considerations must be neglected, but there are two cautions worth considering. First, can the catastrophe really be prevented, and if so, can it be prevented only by this neglect of other considerations?[1] Second, if the heroic treatment of immediate catastrophe leads ultimately to therapists being regarded as tricksters, has the success of many clients with many therapists, at some time in the future, been bartered away for the sake of short-term, dramatic change?

One response to those looking for quick and economical solutions is that serious change is often slow and difficult. Superficial treatment may lead to superficial change, granted that "superficial" is one of those words that has value judgment buried within it. When dramatic change does seem available, the price must be judged in terms that go beyond immediate dollar costs. As suggested earlier, the price in terms of values sacrificed or long term credibility lost might be excessive. Alternatively, individuals with very different priorities than those expressed here might not find the cost to be high at all. As should be clear from what has been said earlier, I have no quarrel with them unless the values they express seem truly horrific or the claim is made that the therapist's personal values are irrelevant.

Perhaps there are many therapists whose attitudes are similar to those expressed here, who take a modest view of what therapists should or can do, and who find themselves in a similar position to the *Bourgeois Gentilhomme*. Moliere's hero was surprised and pleased to find that he had been speaking prose. These therapists may be surprised but not pleased if they find that what they have been doing is now to be called "Minimal Therapy." They are offered apologies and only the following defense. The gimmicky, the dramatic, the technique-oriented therapies tend to be visible, more so than they deserve, in my opinion. Those of us who have seen gimmicks come and go, and who sometimes have had the work of dealing with clients previously treated in these ways, might have some stake in arguments being made, perhaps even repeatedly, for a more modest view.

Consider a seduction. Sam has set out to seduce Sally. He takes some time to consider carefully the strengths and weaknesses of alternative strategies. One possibility is to try the bold approach. He could try a frontal assault, as it were, with vigorous flirtation and humorous but unmistakably sexual innuendos in talk and actions. Clear disdain for social conventions might be expressed. If Sam chooses this strategy, he will hope to titillate and amuse and also to establish himself as a sexual threat and (more important) temptation. This strategy has the advantage of being quick, of being dramatic and fun, and of leaving relatively few early interventions to explain away when the "mark is cooled out." That is, after Sally is seduced, he will not have to explain away any earlier words disclaiming a physical interest in her. If the strategy is successful, Sam will feel himself in control of their interaction almost immediately, and Sally will be off balance, not to regain her footing until she has lost it decisively. If the strategy is unsuccessful, Sam might succeed only in looking ridiculous. This is not a strategy for those who lack the skill and panache to carry it off properly.

A second strategy might be to move in gradually and quietly. The first order of business is to establish trust. Sam must evince an interest in Sally as a person, devoting his conversations to topics that emphasize this fact and avoiding any hint of his true intentions. One small point, Sam reminds himself, is to avoid getting caught eyeing those physical attributes of Sally that he actually has his eye on. His sexuality is to be established in more subtle ways, in stylistic aspects of talking and moving and in avoiding behaviors that would make him seem needy. He does not want to seem like "most men," on the assumption that Sally has already learned to distrust most men and to say no to them. Once having insinuated himself into Sally's favor, the time and place for making a decisive move must be chosen carefully. If the move fails, it is all over, since he is now revealed to be other than what he has claimed. If it is successful, however, who cares? Sally as his lover may even be persuaded that he was just swept away by his feelings, as was she, in spite of his attempts to be better behaved. If Sally decides that she was fooled, the worst that can happen, Sam might feel, is that he only gets to sleep with her once.

Afficionados of seduction may imagine numerous other strategies that Sam could adopt, but only one more is pertinent here. Sam could simply approach Sally, and tell her the truth about how he feels. Who knows, she might say yes. The odds are that Sam will not choose this alternative, because he firmly believes it is less effective than any number of alternative strategies and because results are what count. Is he wrong?

Surely, Ryder does not expect us to take this silly story as a metaphor for the practice of therapy. Well, yes; he does. Here, with its unattractive luster, is the advance planning, the fraud, and the manipulation that characterize some current therapeutic practice. The justification for therapy that has these aspects is the same as Sam's: It works; in fact, it works a lot better than the next best thing, or so it is claimed.

Of course, therapy is for positive objectives, and Sam's goal is not positive. Who says? Therapists have sometimes felt that a client needed a sexual experience and should be encouraged to have one. They believed it was a positive objective. Is Sally harmed by sleeping with Sam? That is, is she harmed by the sexual act itself? Perhaps. She may be much more likely to be harmed by the realization that she has been cynically manipulated, that she has trusted someone who was not to be trusted, that she has been played for a fool. Whatever else is true, Sally has not been treated as if she deserves respect and honesty.

Suppose Sally never realizes that Sam is a fake. Is she harmed then? To put the question in more broad perspective, is a person harmed by being subjected to fraud and manipulation that is never discovered? If these actions in therapy are justified by the claim that clients do not catch on, and therefore no harm is done, perhaps Sam too should be forgiven for everything but incompetence. Unfortunately, it does stick in one's craw a little to say that there is nothing wrong with Sam's endeavor as long as his "clients" never realize what he is doing.

The easiest point to be made about this anecdote is of course that what Sam does is unattractive. A slightly less crass point is that "what Sam does" does not refer to his overt behavior with Sally, at least not at the level of detail described here. It is easy to imagine someone enacting very similar overt behavior (similar enough that a treecounter would find no differences) but without Sam's calculation or duplicity. To say that Sam is a fake is to imagine the possibility of someone doing similar things who is less fake. Sam certainly hopes that Sally imagines such a possibility. No, it is the inner Sam, perhaps the intentional Sam, whose characteristics are decisive in shaping an evaluation of his actions. The characteristics of the inner, intentional Sam also may be decisive, ultimately, in shaping consequences for Sally.

Finally, it is likely that the Sallys of the world are not such fools as Sam imagines. Some will see through Sam right away and either go

along for the ride or not, as they choose. They may even manipulate Sam
with a level of skill greater than his. Others will realize later that they
have been had. Still others may never clearly perceive Sam's calculation
or deception for what it is but may feel a little peculiar about their
relationship with Sam. Somehow it did not feel quite right. Was there
something wrong with me? What did I do that made it fail?

These different ways of seeing the relationship, and of seeing Sam,
may not all be terrible, but all of them contribute to a view of
relationships in general that includes fakery, treachery, or "just" a vague
feeling of emptiness. Also, all of them have parallels in relationships that
are supposed to be therapeutic.

What about the argument that Sally may be asking for it and that
therefore Sam is not so bad? Most of us have learned to dislike this
argument as applied to sexual advances, but what about the same
argument as applied to clients? That is, if a client asks a therapist to do
whatever is in the therapist's power to provide help, is the therapist then
to be blamed for doing exactly as requested, even if the actions intended
to help include trickery? Perhaps there is some merit to this argument,
but it does seem unlikely that most clients understand their request for
help as including a request to be fooled. My own experience with clients
who are themselves therapists is that even therapists who regularly
manipulate others do not want to be manipulated when they themselves
become clients. Even if this argument were correct—that the client's
request for help justifies any action that might help—the problem would
remain of reinforcing a questionable view of relationships in general and
a view of therapy that in the long run might not be in our interest.

What is most enormously unfair about this anecdote is that it neglects
any consideration of caring. Sam differs in an important way from most
therapists not so much in the content of his behavior nor in the content
of what he intends Sally to do. It is rather that Sam's caring is, or is
alleged to be, almost exclusively for Sam. The question is not so much
whether Sally will be hurt but whether Sam gives a damn. He does not,
or claims not to, and we do, or claim to.

Furthermore, the fact of Sam's not caring, or at least of Sam's claim
to himself that he does not care, might make it inevitable that Sally is
hurt in the same way that deception may be harmful. That is, it is not
necessary for Sally to notice consciously that Sam only pretends to care.
If anything, the vague or barely noticed feeling that Sam's caring seems
not to ring true may be more troubling to Sally than a clear perception of
poor Sam as he is.

Inevitably, this fable itself is lacking in the same way that Sam is most lacking. The anecdote itself, as a piece of prose, is uncaring. It is presented in spite of the fact that it must be an affront to some readers and in spite of the possibility that it might cause not just anger but also pain. The overt concern here for caring, as for honesty and respect, does not imply, and is not meant to imply, that the present author himself is beyond criticism in these matters.

It seems likely that almost everyone values caring, although it may be awkward or seem unscientific to mention such a topic in the contemporary clinical literature. Although a corollary concern for therapist honesty and respect for clients is no doubt also widely held, there seem to be large differences in the importance attached to these values and in the implications to be drawn from them. To some extent these are ultimate values not justifiable by an appeal to still more important values that they serve. Still, there are some arguments that can be made, that might make further sense of the fairly extreme position described here.

In eighteenth-century France, when nicer, more gentle treatment of children was urged, the primary argument was not the instrumental one that more decent treatment of children would lead to better adults. The argument was more that many children were fated to die without ever becoming adults. Since the life to be had as a child would be all the life many children would ever experience, it was a matter of simple humanity to provide children with something desirable while they were still around to enjoy it.

The parallel to be drawn for treatment is hardly a matter of life and death but is perhaps nonetheless of some importance. Treatment sometimes is not a great success, even considering a variety of ways to define "success." Considering this fact, which I hope is not controversial, a therapist still has the possibility of providing something of some value. Even if nothing else happens, a therapist is almost always able to provide clients with the opportunity to experience a relationship that is relatively straightforward, and relatively respectful, with a minimum of hidden agendas that the therapist seeks to implement without revealing. All such experiences, wherever they can happen, might well be regarded as valuable and worth some effort.

More than a few people come into treatment feeling that they have never experienced a relatively decent, relatively honest relationship. Now they approach an alleged expert in relationships, perhaps partly with the hope of finding something better for themselves in the future than they have had in the past. If they come to notice that the therapeutic relationship, in spite of all its rudeness and other imperfections, is relatively honest and respectful, relatively free of various kinds of seduction, they see that something better does exist. They may become more likely to notice that "something better" when the opportunity occurs in other settings, even if nothing else happens in therapy.

Clients may also come to perceive, and not as a matter of distortion, that relationships even as managed by experts are manipulative, hokey, and perhaps fake. Even if other positive things happen (the learning of social skills, the abandonment of past grudges, perhaps even some genuine insight), they may then leave therapy with less hope for a decent relationship than they had at the beginning.

We live in a society that is not long on trust. We may do our clients no favor by providing them the opportunity to become still less trusting. In the long run, we may do our profession a similar disservice, as one form or another of therapy becomes known for its trickery. As Goffman (1969) has pointed out, when deception becomes an expectable part of communication, communication itself degenerates and becomes very difficult.

There is another aspect of respect for clients that might be mentioned here, although it will come up again. It is a cliché that happens to be true. Clients have a right to change or not to change as they wish. Therapists, of course, also have the right to lend themselves or not to some particular direction of change. Whatever work is done in therapy is thus in the area of overlap between what clients want and what therapists are willing to assist. The point here is only that it is impertinent of therapists to decide for clients that such and such is what needs to be changed and then to work for that change with or without the clients wanting it.

The power of psychotherapy in helping people change comes from.... This sentence has a number of possible completions, all with some truth to them. For instance, boundary conditions can be cited. People can express the feelings they do in therapy because they trust that in therapy these expressions will not lead to certain kinds of consequences. Therapists can come closer to devoting themselves to other people's interests because they only have to do it for a limited period of time. Some might cite a deliberate disregard of good manners. A therapist may or may not answer questions, may say things that would be rudely blunt in ordinary social intercourse, and in general may fail to cooperate with interpersonal dances that clients employ without previously having paid attention to them. Therapist ambiguity might be cited, as in the well-known "blank screen" that permits unrealistic fantasies to flourish and grow until they become obvious. Analysis of the transference is the real work in therapy, it might be said, with all the rest only being useful by making transference analysis possible. All of these alternatives are probably true, at least in context, although some of the therapist activities they imply can be techniques in the sense that will be criticized here. For the moment, however, the most salient sentence completion is that the particular power of therapy is related to a determined and caring adherence to intentionality as an explanation for the events in people's lives.

Is it really true that most of what individuals, couples, and families do is related to their intentions? Is it really true that most of what people accomplish, whether it seems wanted at first glance or not, is what people have intended to accomplish in some sense? There are two answers, depending on one's (meta) point of view. From the logically prior view of acknowledging that a range of different stands can be taken about what people do, the answer is that the question is wrong. Intentionality is simply a stand that can be taken. The most that can be said for it is that intentionality is a stand that can be made to fit. From the view of actually having taken this stand, the second answer becomes operative, and it is yes.

A therapist's conviction that intentionality is correct as an explanation for client accomplishments (or therapist accomplishments) makes it easier for secret intentions to be acknowledged and for unperceived intentions to be perceived. It helps provide a chance for clients to see their responsibility for their own lives and to pursue some intentions more simply and easily.

What about the opposite point of view, that physical and social forces outside our control shape our lives with precious little regard for what we want and even are the source of our wants? Yes, this is true, too. However, clients tend to be already persuaded of this truth to one extent or another. It is not a truth that provides a chance to see new opportunities within oneself or in the world.

Suppose you have a headache. If the headache seems part of some complex of emotional events that is important to you, it might be worthwhile to consider the fact that this headache is something you are doing and is somehow serving your purposes. Alternatively, the headache may not be that important to you, and your interest in an immediate growth in self-awareness may be nil. You therefore regard the headache as a result of vascular changes related to biochemical processes you do not understand. You do understand that the pain you feel is affected by aspirin, so you take two and go to bed (which may be part of why you had the headache).

A substrate orientation is not ordinarily helpful in therapy if therapy is intended to affect awareness. A substrate orientation is ordinarily of no help at all if therapy is intended to help people see the extent to which they can and do manage their own lives.

Smith comes to see me, or so she says, because her husband told her to. She saw a local psychiatrist some time ago, because of some conversations between herself and her stereo system, but the psychiatrist told her to repair her relationship with her mother. Her husband cannot stand her mother, sees little resemblance between his mother-in-law and the stereo, and therefore told her to quit therapy. Since the stereo is still being conversational, her husband lately has been pushing her to see me. They looked through the phone book together, found my name, liked it (because it sounded Anglo-Saxon), and called me. That is, he dialed the phone and gave it to her when I answered, or so I found out later.

Smith's initial presentation is as a person who has never made an independent decision in her life. Someone has always told her what to do, held her hand while she did it, and then told her that she did it badly. She says that her husband refuses to join her in seeing me. When I suggest that she can get him to come in if she wants to, she looks at me very strangely. I sound, she says, a little like her stereo.

In due course it turns out that the truth is not as initially presented. Smith had the role in her family of being the wise—at least the responsible—fool. Others were in charge, but she saw to it that they did not get their fingers burned too badly while they were at it. Her present life as a spouse is similar, playing the fool while keeping her drunken husband from getting hurt too badly, or abusing the children, or missing time from work. On the side she does what she wants with an almost merry disregard of convention. She has gone through several lovers in the course of her marriage. Separating from her last lover was the occasion for seeking a therapist. The psychiatrist's willingness to pass on her secrets to her husband was her (most overt) reason for quitting. My apparent ethnicity was indeed one reason, it seemed, for picking me, but it was as one of a number of things (my being nonmedical was another) that suggested maximum social distance between me and her previous therapist.

Smith initially came on very strongly as a helpless child looking for guidance and direction. This presentation was not a conscious lie, or if it was, it was as much a lie to herself as to anyone else. Buying this fairy tale would not have been productive.

Brown's wife is unforgiving about his sterility. She would do anything to have a child (except adopt one or employ artificial insemination). What a rotten break for her, she says. It turns out that Brown had a serious case of mumps about two years before marriage, probably the cause of his sterility. His wife knew about the mumps before marrying him, but it is always possible (?) that potential sterility never occurred to her. By the way, the wife is a physician.

Johnson is sitting in his living room when his wife comes home. She shouts and screams at him before he says a word, proving (?) that her unpleasantness is not his fault. It turns out that he had promised to wait up for her, and had done so, but had left the house in total darkness except for the television set in the living room. She was bound to believe that he had broken his promise, until she found him in the living room and realized that she had been set up. A smile grows on Johnson's face as he begins to perceive consciously, and to acknowledge, his pleasure at his wife's subsequent rage. Now that he thinks of it, he recalls sitting in the living room chuckling inwardly in expectation of his wife's reaction at seeing the darkened house.

The terminology here uses terms such as "show" or "see" or "perceive" because they seem appropriate. Therapy as described here is intended to help people experience more of themselves, including feelings that have been locked up out of sight and intentions that may always have been kept invisible. With due apologies to all the others who have said these things first, and with no apologies to those preoccupied with behavior, experiencing something is not the same as being told it exists and is not even the same as believing that it exists. Believing that something exists (in oneself) is even likely to be a way one avoids allowing it into awareness.

Perhaps the only way people learn what insight is like is by experiencing it. Happily enough, it is a common experience.

For many of us, there are times of feeling low, not necessarily for any very obvious reason. We may feel miserable, grumpy, unsociable, and uninterested in anything positive. We really get into it. Some of the people around us may come to believe that we are determined to be as unhappy as possible. Some people might conclude that we are actually enjoying being miserable.

Suppose it dawns on us, perhaps with a giggle, that this is really true. We have worked hard for this low mood, and we are loving it. Reference here is not to an abstract belief that we must be miserable for some purpose but to the conscious experience of the pleasure we are getting. Surely this must have happened, perhaps secretly, for a lot of us.

On the face of it, who could argue with pleasure becoming more conscious? If we are to do something anyway, we might as well get as much satisfaction out of it as possible. Pleasure that is conscious seems, well, more pleasant. The trouble is that when our enjoyment of a bad mood comes into awareness, it becomes much more difficult to maintain the bad mood. Our miseries lack conviction when we are having conscious fun out of them. In other words, not only is the bad mood doing something for us, our lack of awareness is also of use, since it permits a more convincing bad mood. With awareness, we can still play at the bad mood, but the real sting of it is likely to evade our grasp.

Insight is thus not being used to refer to some set of labored historical rationales for present difficulties. Insight is always immediate experience, in the present. This, of course, is what insight has always meant.

As was mentioned in an earlier essay, there is a popular belief that insight is unrelated to behavior change. If observation is careful enough, and if subtle nuances are accepted as behavior, this assertion is probably untrue. Similar behavior may occur, but if the tension behind behavior—the real sting—is gone, it will be slightly different, and its social consequences are likely to be different. In any case, it is not obvious that changed behavior is any of my business. If a client understands and is aware of his or her wants and feelings, how the client chooses to implement intentions is the client's business. If a client's behavior so affronts my conscience that I feel obligated to intervene, or creates a legal obligation that I intervene, so be it. But my intervention in such a case is not therapy as described here. I am acting, in such a case, as a representative of society or of my own conscience and no longer as a representative of the client.

The fundamental fact is that a person cannot consistently regard clients as responsible for their own lives and at the same time claim, in words or deeds, to take responsibility for what they do.

Sam, poor fellow, is not a successful psychopath after all. After numerous unhappy experiences with women, he has become morose, reclusive, and obese. He comes to my office and asks my assistance in losing weight. I offer to help him understand his situation better, if he is seriously interested in doing so, but refuse his request to help him become more slim. Furthermore, if he is interested in my opinion, he might want to be cautious about losing weight before he sees clearly the way his weight is making his life easier. This is not a ploy, by the way, but an expression of honest concern. Also by the way, the opinion expressed is only that. It is not an attempt, or at least not a conscious attempt, to get him to change his mind.

If Sam is really determined to find some external agent that will be responsible for his weight loss, he will go elsewhere and may even lose weight. He may then come back, more ready to believe that what he heard the first time around was the truth.

This attitude to Sam is partly a function of some respect for his right to choose his own life, an unwillingness to lend any support for the view that others can be responsible for him and a respect for whatever is important to Sam about being obese. I am confident that Sam can lose weight without my help, if that is now what he wants to do. Respect for Sam, in other words, dictates that he be treated as if he is an adult human being, which he is chronologically, even if he acts in some ways like a child.

It has been suggested elsewhere in these essays that there is something more richly human, in effect, in a person being regarded as intentional and less human in being seen from a substrate point of view. From a substrate point of view, using Anthony Burgess's phrase, a person can come to seem like a clockwork orange. To regard a client (or a family, dyad, etc.) as a complicated cybernetic machine is not only to regard her/him/them as a little less than fully human, but probably is also to regard the client(s) as less human than the therapist(s). Even when therapists regard clients from a substrate orientation, they seem to characterize their own actions largely as expressions of their intentions.

Human reality viewed as intentional, a high evaluation of honesty and respect, and awareness as a primary goal are therefore the premises on which this therapy is based. It will turn out that an extreme view is taken here of these three positions. The conclusions drawn may go beyond those drawn by others with similar values. For the moment, it is mainly pertinent to emphasize that these three positions are closely related to each other. To a certain extent they imply each other.

Among other things, respect means regarding someone as fully human. To the extent that a person is seen as a fancy machine, that person is a little diminished. Respect and intentionality are thus tied together. To respect a person means, among other things, acknowledging and not interfering with that person's right and capability to make decisions, to manage his or her own life. To support intentionality consistently, a therapist cannot contribute to the fiction that she or he (the therapist) is partly responsible for a client's behavior. Thus both respect and intentionality argue, in effect, for not attempting to coerce, manipulate, or even influence client behavior. Helping clients in the clients' efforts to see their lives more clearly, and the ways these lives are the work of their own hands, thus seems best for serving an emphasis on respect and intentionality. It is even, to use the trite phrase, "growth inducing" in the sense that becoming more aware of oneself as an intentional being is becoming more fully a person.

Most of us have stark terrors buried within ourselves as individuals and ideas that would seem crazy if brought out into the light of day. The same is true of couples and families. Many therapists believe that if therapy goes far enough, it eventually means becoming aware of, facing, experiencing some of these terrors and ideas. Perhaps this kind of thing is not related to intentionality, or perhaps it is. What people most fear seems always to be also most wanted. In any case, it is not necessary to insist that all growth in awareness is a matter of intentionality. It is enough to suggest that intentionality is an organizing focus not to be lost sight of. Attention to awareness is most likely to enhance a person's conscious grasp of his or her own life and (compared to alternatives) seems least likely to send out the message that a therapist is willing, as many others may have been, to assume charge over what the person does or perhaps even feels.

There are a number of implications to be drawn from all this at a level of specificity that becomes a little more idiosyncratic. Some of these may seem almost trivial, as in the question of what to call clients. This is not the question of whether to call them clients, patients, or customers. The question is whether Sam Samson gets to be called Sam, Mr. Samson, or something else. If a client is to be treated with respect, and if there is a sense in which the client is the one in charge of what happens, and if therapy is not a social friendship, Sam Samson should be addressed as Mr. Samson. It seems a bit belittling, a bit talking down, to address a client by her or his first name. There is also something a little disrespectful about referring to adult family members as "Mom" and "Dad" the way nurses do on obstetrical wards.

If "Dr. Smith" tells "Sally" that she is an adult person, it is possible that "Sally" might not be persuaded that "Dr. Smith" is persuaded that the statement is true. It is not necessarily a great help if "Dr. Smith" becomes plain "Jane" and both parties collude at being social friends.

There are a number of other things therapists can do that seem (to me) to indicate disrespect for clients as serious human beings, even though no deception may be involved and no belittling terminology may be used. Basically, anything hokey falls into this category. If clients are told to go home, go into their backyard, and fight it out with water pistols, this is hokey. Various testing procedures might seem similarly hokey, or at least mysterious. Clients are asked to take on faith that some arcane procedure looks into their interior in a way that shows professionals what the clients themselves cannot see and that may not be explained. Not only can such procedures be demeaning, they can help to foster a view of other persons being in charge of the clients' lives.

One popular and sometimes demeaning activity is the demonstration that involves putting clients in front of an audience so that the assembled throng can see how some visiting expert works with them. The educational value of this procedure may be great. It may even appeal to client narcissism. It is difficult to find in it respect for clients' worth and maturity. It seems to trivialize one of the most serious endeavors of a client's lifetime by turning it into a show.

Much the same comments apply to the popular practice of video-taping sessions or observing them through one-way windows. Trusting a therapist and engaging in an honest therapeutic relationship is difficult enough for a client without being asked to relate to a window, a camera, and some unseen collection of whomevers. Is a client to believe that the entire organization being dealt with has a respectful attitude to the client and to the therapy? Is a client to believe that the therapist's actions are really meant for the client and are not partly meant to communicate over the client's head to the observers? That is, is not a therapist only partly doing therapy while in part the therapist is showing off something (sometimes even the client) to unseen others? Tapes may be great for training or for research. It is doubtful that they are great for therapy, if therapy is to be construed as fundamentally a very serious and very personal human relationship.

I remember my first training (as a professional) in nonverbal communication. Sound recordings were being made of my sessions and it dawned on me that I was working at getting messages across to clients without my supervisor finding out. (Yes, she found out anyway.)

Joe and Suzy (a married couple) sit down with their therapist, Harry. Harry is being supervised by Tom as part of a class being taken also by Carol, George, Marge, and Marlene. At the beginning of a session, Joe and Suzy turn to the camera and say, "Hi, Tom. Hi, folks." And good night Mrs. Calabash, wherever you are.

There are any number of things a therapist can do to establish himself or herself as being in charge of clients' lives, to one degree or another. Charismatic Max comes sweeping into the consulting room, with an all but visible cape around his shoulders. His presence seems to fill the room. In a commanding manner he then engages clients in a variety of activities that mystify them, puzzle them, and totally unhinge their usual defensive maneuvers. All the while he delivers a patter that stresses unyieldingly that they are totally responsible for their own lives. His nonverbal communication thus grossly contradicts the words he says and is likely to make a greater impact.

Charismatic therapy, therapy with arcane procedures that make sense to the doctor but not to the clients, and any kind of authoritarian therapy—all these are ruled out. It is true that they can be fun, and that they puff up therapist narcissism, but they also contribute, from the point of view of present values, to one of the clients' central problems in living. They assert, regardless of what is said in words, that the therapist is largely in charge of changes in clients' lives. A client can pick up, without being told, that her or his life is, still, partly the work of someone else's hands.

So-called homework assignments can have the same implication. Whatever else they accomplish, they establish (and are probably meant to establish) the therapist as a force that imposes itself on clients' lives. The present view is that clients need to see more clearly how much their lives are their own. Telling them what to do when they get home diminishes rather than enhances their stature as people, and particularly so if what they are told to do is silly.

Exercises carried out in the consulting room are also a problem from this point of view. Any directive whatsoever given by a therapist to clients is likely to constitute a message, to one extent or another, that the therapist is in charge of what clients do. Directives thus, other things being equal, hinder clients in coming to see (not just to believe) the extent to which they, the clients, are in charge of what they do.

It might be useful at this point to make a distinction between manipulation and influence. As used here, the former term involves some fraud. Actions are taken for purposes that are deliberately hidden from clients or presented as being for purposes that are actually untrue. Manipulation is a kind of influence, but influence can also be straightforward. If a therapist directs a client to meet with her former husband, there may be no fakery about the therapist's purposes. However, even without manipulation, this still seems to be an example of the therapist asserting some responsibility for the client's life.

Moving on to more formidable targets, the medical establishment as a whole may be a handicap to therapy of this sort. It provides a context that would seem to communicate messages opposite to those advocated here.

Medical practice is often dehumanizing in its determinedly substrate orientation toward patients and in its sweeping assumptions of responsibility. Generally speaking, the doctor will decide what the doctor is to do, and the doctor will decide what the patient is to do, sometimes without a sensible explanation.

The sort of therapy described here has seemed less easy in a medical setting and it may be less easy if a therapist is identified primarily as a physician. It seems sad that socially oriented therapists, physicians or not, may sometimes find it necessary to mimic a "scientific" substrate view, perhaps including a reification of "illness," and the idea that the therapist knows best.

Therapeutic techniques in general have a number of unfortunate features. One is that they can be manipulative in the sense mentioned above. Consider an easy one, "active listening." A person consciously carrying out this technique restates what a client has just said and asks if the restatement is accurate. If successful, active listening leaves a client feeling that the therapist is concerned about him or her, and wants to be sure that the client has been accurately understood. The therapist's reality may be quite different, in that the therapist's intention is to do therapy and one of the things one does in therapy is active listening. The reason for doing active listening is that it "makes" clients feel the way just described. The therapist is thus evincing interest that may not exist or that may exist but not have much to do with the evincing behavior that the therapist has been taught to enact.

Generally speaking, active listening depends for its success on the receiver of this technique not knowing that this technique is being used. Its effect depends, in other words, on the client being fooled.

Hazel is a student nurse required to take a course on "communication skills." The course has a small group format in which students learn about "skills" and practice them. One day, Hazel has a serious traffic accident on her way to class and narrowly escapes without injury. She goes on to class, quite upset, and arrives late. The instructor suggests that since Hazel is upset and needs calming, this would be a fine opportunity for the class to practice its active listening skills on her. The class proceeds to do as instructed, and Hazel becomes furious. Should anyone be surprised?

Joe and Georgia are a married couple. They also train people in interpersonal techniques, including active listening. When Georgia gets angry at Joe, he tries active listening. Georgia says, "Don't you active listen me, you son of a bitch."

Techniques may vary in terms of how much they depend on fooling clients, but many of them have at least one aspect of deception in common, namely, that they purport to come from the therapist. In fact, there is a sense in which they do not come from the person who is, at that particular moment, playing therapist. They come from some textbook someplace, or some classroom, or some workshop, or some planning session, or even some ideological formulation. In a sense, the therapist as a person immediately present in the room is only a conveyance.

This is really what is meant here by technique—a building block, an objectified thing, that can be employed when the situation seems right. As such, there is a sense in which the therapist hides behind techniques. If successful, the therapist him or herself may never be directly seen— "found out" is a better expression—by the client.

The consequences of technique, as that term is now being used, cover the full range of Sally's reactions to Sam the seducer. Anger at manipulation, or at attempts at fakery, feeling not treated with respect or genuineness, or just feeling vaguely that something hollow is going on, are all possible. The client may even feel encouraged to play the same game in return, leading to some very strange therapeutic interaction.

Even openness can be used as a technique in this sense of putting distance between the therapist and the client. Apart from the intrusiveness of therapist self-revelations and other complications they bring, they can also be something for the therapist to hide behind or to use for fending off the clients. Nakedness, after all, can be a very flashy and eye-catching costume that seriously hinders one's perception of whatever else may be going on.

Therapist fears are a real fact of life, and therapists surely have a right to protect themselves when they feel it necessary. The unfortunate inevitability of self-protection, however, need not be confused with providing the best possible interpersonal situation.

If techniques are to be frowned upon taken one at a time, their orchestration into a coherent strategy for arranging change must be favored even less.

Informal use of the concept of hypnosis seems to be acquiring a degree of currency these days as a way of understanding some family therapy. Some dance is done by the therapist(s) that induces a suggestible state in the family, and then a more decisive therapeutic move is made (something like the second strategy considered by Sam in his pursuit of Sally). This may be a useful metaphor without necessarily being a compliment. Hypnosis traditionally refers to an arrangement in which two parties convince themselves that the intentionality of one of them (the hypnotist) controls both of them. From the point of view of the controllee, this is not helpful in facilitating an awareness of oneself (individual, couple, or family) being the author of one's own life.

Even from the point of view of the therapist, control-oriented technique strategies are a dubious benefit. Success affirms that one is in control, but in so doing success (over another person) affirms also that dependency and catastrophe, if there is loss of control, are omnipresent possibilities in human relationships.

One last aspect of a technique, in the sense used here, is that it is defined by therapist purposes, not by the particular behavior employed. It might be possible to note stylistic aspects of behavior, such as a certain stereotyped quality, that might give something away as being a technique, but basically a technique is defined by processes inside the therapist.

A therapist looks a family in the eyes (as much as possible) and tells them that they are instructed to do such and such. Such and such turns out to be exactly what the family came in complaining about. Perhaps the therapist has just taken on some responsibility for family behavior. Perhaps the therapist has just employed a well-known technique, prescribing the symptom. If a supervisee told me this story, my initial guess probably would be that these two things were what happened. But there might be another version that is more accurate. Perhaps the therapist knows this family so well as to be confident that the family will realize, after a shocked moment or two, that they are being spoofed. The therapist might be telling the family something, in a way that they will hear, about how much the family members not only are, but also want to be, in charge of their own craziness.

After seeing Jack for some time, Jack tells me that he wants me to stop him from smoking dope. I agree, and ask him how much he smokes in an average evening. The answer is, "Six or eight joints." After being suitably impressed with his volume of consumption, I instruct Jack to go home this evening and smoke exactly seven joints. Jack then has a temper tantrum for about five minutes, in which he tells me to butt out of his life. When it is over, I am confident that he has gotten my point.

Before continuing with this line of thought, it might be useful to distinguish this discussion from reframing. Suggesting that the world looks different from different points of view, several of which can be accurate in their own terms, is not the same as suggesting that all characterizations of the world are accurate (in any terms). Reframing connotes to me the idea that any characterization can be pressed into service if it seems desirable and that considerations of its accuracy are secondary at best. For example, it connotes the possibility of therapists telling clients things that they (the therapists) do not believe. Reframing seems usually to refer to an act, a technique, that may or may not reflect its user's actual frame of reference. Suggesting that similar appearing things are different if internal reality is different, involves neither reframing nor a shifting point of view. Practical difficulty in determining which potential internal reality is closer to the truth does not change the fact that, given some point of view, there may be a truth out there.

Notice, however, what is going on here. This line of thought pulls the rug out from under me. A "disapproved list" of things not to do is provided in the preceding paragraphs. Most of these things are described in terms of overt events. Now it must be acknowledged that this list is based on guesses about probable internal realities of therapists, and meanings probably conveyed to clients. To the extent that these guesses are wrong, the list becomes nonsense.

A distinction between behavior and internal reality is put nicely in this quote from Kaiser (1965):

> I remember a lecture about the technique of therapy. We all raved about this lecture. . . . It was a pleasure to listen to him. . . . He said that the therapist should . . . use tact and delicacy. For instance, he said, when the patient is just in the process of revealing a painful secret you would not light your cigar!

> When I heard this I found it very plausible and felt sure I would never light a cigar when the patient was about to reveal a painful secret! Yet, when I remember after so many years, this simple humane advice I am not as convinced as I was with regard to its validity. If you are paying attention to the patient, if you are *with* [the patient], as I would like to say, you might not even notice whether you are lighting your cigar or not—and it does not matter! Whenever you feel the need to do something, or to refrain from doing something for the purpose of showing [the patient] your concern, you can be certain that your concern is lacking.

Genuineness is not simply a role that one can adopt. A neophyte therapist reading this essay in a suitably impressionable mood might follow carefully the do's and don't's that seem (to such a reader) to be found here, and yet end up doing the kinds of things to which objection is being taken. Doing things because they seem required by some ideology is flirting closely with playing a part, that is, not being very real.

It is easy to imagine exceptions, but usually it is better for a therapist to do something stupid and honest than to do something clever and deceptive. In the former case there may be at least more trust available afterward so that the therapist might be listened to when he or she does better on another day. Other things equal, or even moderately unequal, without trust there is less likely to be another day.

For example, one might read this as an advocacy of unconditional positive regard, not only toward clients but also toward client behavior, since anything else might look like influencing client behavior. This would be wrong, unless the therapist is such a bland and/or saintly person that unconditional positive regard is always what is happening. Ms. Smith asks me if I think she is crazy for walking up five flights of stairs to my office instead of taking the elevator (as her husband does). I might not answer, but if I do respond to the question as it is put, it is hard to imagine an honest, nonevasive answer that does not boil down to yes.

Bill says, "When I leave here, I am going home to shoot my wife. I have the revolver here in my pocket. Since you are sworn to confidentiality, you can do nothing. Right?" Is there anyone out there who would not consider outright lying in such a case? The therapist who told me this story did lie, got the client out of his office, and then called the police. The point is not just that telling the truth might have been a little dumb. There might be situations in which lying is more genuinely humane, perhaps in a sense even more honest, than an unrealistic devotion to the truth. Paradoxically, in such a case lying might even increase a client's trust in the therapist being a real person.

Suppose a client says that she or he is going to commit suicide. If the client alone is responsible for the client's life, is the client to understand that the therapist will stand by and permit this act? I think so. People have a right to self-destruction. Furthermore, promises of rescue attempts, or having a history of actual rescues, or even hints that these facts might be true, can convey the impression that the therapist will be responsible for preserving the client's life with consequences that might be accidentally fatal. Far from being a basis for moving away from minimal therapy, the possibility of suicide makes clear and simple honesty, and clarity about who is responsible for what, become matters of urgent importance.

Other than the possibility of exceptional situations, there are several issues that raise questions about the therapy described here. Some of them are discussed below, including blaming the victim, complications if the client is a couple or family, shifting point of view, and consistency problems with an extreme intentionality position.

Suppose an individual client is a member of some group that society has placed at a serious disadvantage. She, let us say, is black or Hispanic. Suppose further that the unhappiness described by this person consists largely of complaints about situations and events that are related to these facts. In short, she is a serious victim of sex and ethnic discrimination. If a therapist insists on her responsibility for her own life, is not he, let us say, doing this thing that has become known as blaming the victim?

He might be, but not necessarily. Consider an example that is less politicized and that is not necessarily a matter of therapy. Joe is a professional boxer who has been losing lately. We might take Joe to one side and tell him that we can teach him to do better. If he learns to do better, he might still lose, but probably less often and with less humiliating thoroughness. The first point is thus that noticing Joe not to be as good a fighter as he might be is not the same thing as blaming him for losing. On the contrary, Joe must acknowledge that he is not doing as well as he might as a prerequisite for improving.

It turns out that Joe has learned, without paying much attention to it, that there are ways in which he can use this business of losing. After all, if he is going to lose, he might as well get as much out of it as possible. He can feel brave, because he is, or self-sacrificing, and can rally others to his cause. A lot of people favor an underdog. If any of this is true, Joe might as well pay attention to it, because if he does not, he is not likely to be as good a fighter as he could be. The second point is thus that ignoring any of the reasons Joe's fighting manages not to be as good as it could be is not necessarily doing Joe any favor.

It is a clinical commonplace that most of us learn to make use of our misfortunes so that even misfortunes come to include ways in which some of our interests are satisfied. To see better the ways that this might be true is not the same as saying that society is really all right, or should be left alone. On the contrary, clients may become better fighters, like Joe. Everyone fights better, if that is what they want to do, when they can see what they are doing.

Finally, none of this means that Joe is doing anything wrong. He has a right to get as much as he can out of his situation. He is not reprehensible for taking pride in his bravery.

Marie walks home from work alone at night through a rough neighborhood. She knows that her chances of getting hurt are greater than if she spent the small amount a taxi would cost. Thus there is a sense in which it is true that Marie has chosen to increase her personal danger. There is no reason to jump from this to the moralism that would criticize her for any harm that comes to her, much less the simple-minded view that a potential attacker is therefore less to blame for his attack. Perhaps Marie is perfectly aware of her situation but refuses to be pushed off the street. She might have any number of reasons, such as an interest in self-respect, or in encouraging others by her example. It seems particularly odd for Marie to be a potential object of criticism in a society that usually values bravery. Generally speaking, blame relates to whether a person seems justified in some action, not just to the fact that the action has been freely chosen and hence serves some intentions. It does not even depend on whether or not all the intentions are noble.

Midge Dector (1972) once wrote a book called *The New Chastity and Other Arguments against Women's Liberation.* Her line of attack generally seemed to be that feminists had a mixed bag of personal motives for their ideologies, including some that were not laudable. So? If what Dector said were true, it would only mean that feminists were like everyone else. Such views are only irrelevant to questions of whether discrimination exists and should be halted.

Issues of thinking in terms of individuals, dyads, or larger groups were discussed in an earlier essay. As implied, one might readily move around among perceptual stances. Regarding a dyad or family, plus therapist, as one beast often seems to be the most attractive choice, and in some ways is easier than a more segmental view; but distinctions along these lines are not central to the issues discussed in the present essay, with one exception.

What in the world does insight mean for a dyad or family? Needless to say, this is not such an easy question to answer. One reason it is difficult to address, however, may be because I am necessarily speaking here as an individual. As author, I do not construe myself primarily as a piece of a family and expect that most readers will not construe me primarily as a piece of some multipede (in this context). Suppose, however, I were a group. Suppose, in other words, that the author of this set of essays were the Ryder family (or some other label that would identify us as a family group). If we then wrote sentences such as, "We understand that" or, "We see very clearly," or, "We feel great about," it seems likely that readers would not, for the most part, feel mystified. It would be understood in some way that, say, the Ryder family does have these perceptions and is aware of these feelings, probably without confusing the "we" in these sentences with the so-called imperial we. Faculty members who seem to have a strongly individualist point of view refer regularly to the perceptions and attitudes of the "University Administration" without blinking an eye.

In an actual therapy situation, when the family (or the family plus therapist) is phenomenologically one entity, there are times when awareness seems to dawn on the collectivity. When the family, say, itself seems to have a self-perception that refers to one entity, awareness that dawns seems to pertain to the collectivity in ways that transcend the simple possibility that each individual has greater awareness. Indeed, each individual may not have greater awareness. Whether this perception is therapist fantasy or not, the various things that accompany it are the same for groups as for individuals. That is, there is likely to be affect released, tension abruptly reduced, and ties between individuals that appear both closer and less rigid. If this is fantasy, it is at least pleasant fantasy.

One alleged aspect of insight in an individual is that different portions of the psyche communicate more freely with each other. An analogous process seems to occur with, say, family awareness, in that family secrets (perhaps already known to each family member) can become available to the family as an assembled entity along with the affect that is bound up with these secrets.

Shifts in point of view, and hence differing accounts of events, are likely within the context of minimal therapy somewhat apart from the question of whether there is an individual or some nonindividual focus. Attending to the client, within this context, leads to an account of client and even some therapist material in which what happens flows, directly or indirectly, from client intentions. This point of view is not more "true" than some other point of view, or less so. It is simply a point of view that is useful to the extent that the overriding purpose of therapy is an increased understanding of clients.

Attending to the therapist as the party of primary concern takes one to an account in which much of what happens, even some of the same material, is seen to flow from therapist intentions (conscious or otherwise). Supervision of therapeutic work may go this second route.

The situation is the same as that described in an earlier essay, in which it was noted that aspects apparently of one family member might plausibly be regarded as information about that person, information about the family as a whole, or information about other family members. Here it is suggested that a person adopting the point of view of a therapist may regard actions or feelings of anyone in the therapeutic situation, including those of the therapist(s), as information about the client party. Without contradiction, a supervisor might regard the same material, plus whatever happens in the supervisory situation, as information about the therapist.

Once again, the unproductive appearance of factual disagreement, and much confusion, can result from not paying attention to changes in the point of view from which observations are being made.

There are two subtopics under the general heading of consistency problems that arise with an intentionality orientation. First, if people do and are what they choose, and therapists should not or cannot impose unwanted change, how is therapeutic change to be characterized? Second, how is an intentionality orientation to be squared with the strongly felt experience of trying hard to change, and failing?

Taking these issues in reverse order, "trying" is very different from "doing." George is not very happy about facing a new day. He lies in bed after the alarm goes off trying mightily to get up. Trying will not do it at all. After a while, George gives up on trying and does something much more simple. He just puts one foot on the floor and then the other and actually gets up. George could also quit trying and stay in bed for a while, but it might be difficult to do so without finding some alternative way to rationalize his horizontal position.

After George does get up and dressed, it turns out that his car will not start. By pushing as hard as he can, George pushes his car half a block down the street to a garage.

In both parts of this anecdote, trying refers to the phenomenology of pushing against an obstacle. However, in the first part it appears that both the pushing and the obstacle are plausibly viewed as parts of what George is up to. They are wedded together as an exercise in frustration and an excuse to stay in bed. It is this kind of trying (or way of viewing trying) that seems most prominent (or pertinent) in therapy. A person tries mightily to change and does not. Spouses do almost anything to change each other except what might actually work. Intense efforts to straighten out a delinquent adolescent get nowhere.

Accepting one's intentionality can feel, paradoxically, like giving up and accepting helplessness. One actually is giving up the trying as well as the self-imposed obstacles that are an essential component of this kind of trying. An internal obstacle of this sort tends to be viewed as an alien something within oneself, as "it" rather than as "me." Thus, another part of what may be given up is some part of a phenomenological split between an intentional "I" and an "it" that is an aspect of oneself viewed as substrate. Sound familiar?

The idea of trying seems almost logically to imply some aspect of a substrate orientation. There must be something felt to be external to the intentional "I," and not part of what one is choosing, that provides resistence. Adding only slightly to a traditional orientation, it might be mentioned that the "something" in question might be partly a matter of individual unconscious process, of activity by a spouse, and/or of activity by other family members.

As has been suggested elsewhere in these essays, giving up on futile trying might be followed by an experience of greater effectiveness. This sequence can be regarded either as a causal chain or as "merely" descriptive. To regard it as a causal chain in the clinical situation is likely to be another way to regard part of oneself as substrate. The idea is that a "how to" has been discovered. The intentional part of a person (couple, family), that is, the part regarded as "I," chooses the "how to" (in this case, giving up on futile trying), which is then supposed to have a causal effect on the substrate parts ("it" or perhaps "she/he/them"). An account that is more self-consistent in terms of intentionality would be that a client party has experienced, accepted, or changed his/her/their intentions, a process that includes the phenomenological sequence described above.

The process can also be described as being like the phenomenology of a successful romance. One abandons trying, lets go of control or is swept away from it, only to find a richer life in which one has far more capability.

This distinction between accounts is not merely a matter of philo-sophical niceties. The distinction is between clients attempting to outsmart their own intentions, which usually fails, and clients (individual or otherwise) coming to experience themselves as more unified, intentional, and free.

Consider the stand that virtually all aspects of a person's life are chosen in one way or another. That is, they all serve some set of intentions or another. If therapy then is mostly a matter of becoming aware of this intentionality, does it amount to no more than a realization that the client does not really want to change? Worse yet, if awareness itself (an aspect of client life, certainly) is also as it is to serve client intentions, why should a client be interested in greater awareness? Why should a client be interested in any successful changing at all?

This partly may be a logical contradiction, perhaps even a paradox, that is unfixable. Alternatively, "change" as in greater awareness is at a different logical level than other change. To think of increased awareness as a kind of change seems to involve a subtle movement in point of view. An observer steps outside the framework of minimal therapy, as it were, and regards it from some more inclusive epistemological orientation.

Even without getting into the matter of different logical levels, there may be ways to make a little sense out of therapeutic change within an intentionality orientation.

If clients' awareness at present serves their intentions, is not an increase in awareness a change that is against their wishes? Perhaps so, at least to some extent. It is reasonable to suppose that if client intentions had not lately come to include an interest in change, a client would not have entered therapy. If the wishes did not include, or at least come rapidly to include, an interest in increased awareness, a client would not stay. The point of course is that there is change over time, with or without therapy, including change in what people want, and change in people's interest in awareness.

To some extent therapy is like midwifery. That is, the therapist helps delivery along, but this help is useless if the baby is not already pressing to be born.

So this is minimal therapy, such as it is. Most of its aspects are pretty traditional, although there may be a few points here and there that are different. Imagine writing a lengthy essay on therapy and not once mentioning either Freud or systems theory. There. Now I have mentioned them. Both, of course, are implicit in much of what has been said.

If work is done in the ways suggested here, the satisfactions associated with less restrictive approaches to therapy are bound to be less, not to mention the real accomplishments for clients that less restrictive approaches might bring more readily. Those who feel more or less as I do have looked at these things and, in effect, have looked at their price tags, and have decided that their cost was too great.

If I have seemed to disrespect those who have chosen otherwise, I should apologize, and do so. The apology, if required, is not only for rudeness, but for having failed to be clear. What makes this essay both possible and required is precisely the fact that things look different to different observers, that there are always a number of plausible points of view for any situation, and that everyone, even including therapists, must make his or her own decisions about what positions to take.

In terms of the substance of the present point of view, I hope that at least the point has been made that price tags need to be considered, and that at least some time some prices may be too high.

Perhaps too the point has been made that even with one therapist hand tied behind the back, change can sometimes occur. There are satisfactions to be found within the restrictive framework described here.

A family comes in because of complaints about the youngest child, a 10-year-old boy who is said to be morose and hostile at school. It seems that at home this boy can do no right. He is criticized for how he sits, how he speaks, his table manners, his noisiness, and many other things. There is also an older boy, a fair-haired, attractive child of 14 who seems young for his age and who is treated very gingerly by the family. The deadly secret in this family turns out to be that the older boy has a terrible disease and is not expected to survive adolescence.

A year later, the family is still together, and the older boy is still waiting to die. Now, however, the family grief and fear is more open and shared and seems somehow less paralyzing. There is more weeping than there was earlier, but also more laughing and more warmth. The so-called IP is still criticized, but the criticism has a different flavor. Once the criticism felt like an almost tangible urge to kill. Now it is almost a game, with all parties chuckling about it from time to time. There is some mutual forgiveness for each other's frailties in a situation that the family knows it cannot escape. A casual observer might see little change. After all, the major difference is only between feeling and a bitter refusal to feel.

Note

1. Cervantes has his pair of heroes rescue a child being beaten. They forcibly restrain the man doing the beating and punish him. They then ride off to their next good deed, leaving the child to his fate. It is possible that some well-intentioned efforts at dramatic clinical intervention are similar. A rare published acknowledgement, in which negative results of this kind are described, is by Berman (1973).

11

THERAPY AND RELATIONSHIP POLITICS

These days, a male professional might very well say that he supports feminist values and objectives. He will probably not be very specific about what it is he supports, but he might add more detail either pridefully or humbly. If prideful, he might assert long-standing, pioneering support and a share of credit for past accomplishments. If humble, he might confess past error, thank those who have helped him, and express hope for further help and growth in the future.

All these statements may be true. What is not likely to be true is that they are presented primarily to inform the reader or listener. More likely, their actual purpose is to protect their author from criticism.

Some male professionals are afraid and want strongly not to be condemned. Me, too. So here, too, the reader might want to watch for self-vindication in the guise of other things. The mundane but important fact is that when human relationships become dialectical (as between women and men, racial and ethnic groups, Left and Right, parents and children), strong passions hinder discourse. Discussing issues of guilt and blame and counter-blame, while being personally caught up with these feelings, is a little complicated.

A few years ago I heard complaints about the way a male faculty member lectured on the subject of rape. One particular was that he referred to rapists as offenders, rather than as rapists. His terminology was held to be a political act, a refusal to acknowledge the viciousness of the crime committed and those who committed it.

More recently, I heard a therapist complain that fathers who had committed incest were being referred to as offenders. Here, however, the complaint was that these persons' status as fathers was being ignored or denied. In this therapist's (his) view, the human possibilities for helping troubled people were being hindered by a process of condemnation and dismissal. Offender is thus too harsh for some and not sufficiently harsh for others.

Therapists who work with married couples are inclined to think of blame as a kind of social disease. It must be removed, transcended, or gone around if the spouses are to change back from adversaries to lovers. Is this true? If so, is it a more general truth? Is it generally or often true that somehow disposing of blame, somehow nullifying it, is a precondition for a better life? To put it another way, are therapists well advised to think of blame just as a well-deserved response to degrading and damaging treatment or might they also consider blame as a part of the damage done, as something that harms its owner whether or not it harms the person who is its object?

It would be easy to dismiss this unpalatable view of blame as simply a way to let vicious criminals off the hook, for the sake, no less, of the victim. But what if the alternative is to punish the victim for the sake of punishing the criminal?

No doubt a therapist might support a client in letting go of blame even if the therapist personally dislikes the object of the blame. But it seems doubtful that a therapist who is personally much caught up in blame could be very helpful in this process or would want to be.

Adopting a moral or ethical attitude toward other people's actions is neither correct nor incorrect. It is a point of view, and one may adopt it or not without making a factual error. Some of us might find it desirable or even obligatory (as a matter of ethics concerning our own actions) to maintain this point of view as therapists. Since others will find it obligatory not to do so, a serious debate is possible. What is not sensible is to take a conclusion from a moral point of view, pit it against a conclusion from some other point of view, and try to decide which one is correct.

Asserting that incest in the Smith family is used to hold the family together may be simply silent on the question of morality. There is no immediate moral content in asserting that families act as organized systems in which all the actors play their parts. It is then simple nonsense to go on and assert that Jane is not really a victim because both she and her victimizer are part of the same family system. From one point of view the first part of this assertion has a truth value, and from another point of view the second part has a truth value. They do not conflict; they exist in two different frames of reference.

Individualized blame or not, therapy is literally pointless without value judgment. Even if we as therapists were up to absolutely nothing, we would in effect be voting for doing nothing as desirable conduct. Since we also have values about values, it follows that we will not find all values equally desirable as guides for therapy (see also Ryder, 1986). As should be clear by now, these essays express the extreme but not unusual view that, basically, clients should be what they want to be. If what they want is unacceptable to the therapist, the therapist should not provide service. Is this simply avoiding social responsibilities? Are therapists responsible for not supporting arrangements thought to be oppressive and/or for working to eliminate these arrangements?

Put in the abstract, the first of these questions seems fairly simple. That is, there is no conflict between the idea that we should not seek to create or maintain any social arrangements for our clients and the idea that we should not seek to maintain oppressive arrangements. In practice, of course, we all take some things for granted that might well concern us more. We might find on reflection that taking aspects of the status quo for granted is not so easily distinguished from helping maintain the status quo. We will come back to this, in effect, with some discussion of ideology as providing a changed way of seeing.

The second question is less easy in the sense that the obvious answer may not be very welcome. No, we should not be maneuvering people and families into more desirable social arrangements. We should not be playing God at such a level. There are three aspects to this answer.

First, most of us may believe that maneuvering of a sort by the larger society is the source of the problem we would like to address. If we join society's game but for different purposes, we might well be accused of only becoming better puppeteers for people who to some extent are still puppets. This would be an improvement and a change at one level, but at a broader level might only help to maintain the social status quo.

Second, there is a fundamental difference between working to advance values that can be stated out loud, values that are consensual among therapist and clients, and working to advance values about which clients have not been consulted and which some clients may not support. For example, setting out to boost the stock of one spouse while reducing the stock of the other is not a process both spouses are likely to seek. Creating more proper social distance among family members might not win unanimous support if family members were consulted.

Seeking some goals may require that clients not be consulted, even if the clients would likely support them. A behaviorally oriented psychiatrist listens to a woman talk about her husband and her lover. He brightens up, systematically and by design, whenever she says positive things about her husband or negative things about her lover, and otherwise is glum and unresponsive. The therapy works, but only as long as the client is unaware of what is happening. She must be fooled into believing that there is some genuine quality to the therapist's actions that in truth does not exist. If the therapist explains his intentions in sufficient detail, she will not be fooled, and the process will fail. The family therapy field includes a veritable treasure trove of clever ways to influence people, ways that depend on the clients not understanding what the therapist is up to.

This is the third point. Maneuvering people into a lifestyle thought better by the therapist is likely to require fraud and manipulation, even if we all agree that the lifestyle sought would be an improvement. Here is Jane, manipulated and deceived all her life, and usually not taken seriously as a person. If then we manipulate and deceive her (for her betterment), are we taking her seriously as a person? Are we treating her respectfully?

Insight is one of the usual fruits of adapting a consistent point of view, of taking a stand. Once Darwin had been heard, "survival of the fittest" began to be a more visible aspect of familiar facts. After Freud, those who pursued his thought most avidly saw unconscious processes and sexual symbolism in places where these had not been seen previously. Socialism provided a way of seeing and, hence, insights that had not been noticed previously. The social ferment of the early 1960s increased racial and ethnic awareness dramatically for those whom this ferment touched. Feminism, too, depending as do these others on the extent to which one pursues it, is in part a changed way of seeing that includes new insights.

Insight is used here in a very regular sense, even though this is not a discussion about psychotherapy process. A person has the experience that X perception *appears* to be Y, but turns out *actually* to be Z. For instance, a psychotherapeutic episode with a male therapist and a female client seems to be a matter of personal growth for the client but turns out actually to be a reinforcement of how to be a docile daughter. The "aha" experience, and immediately "knowing" the validity of the experience, mark it as an insight, although not necessarily an insight of the kind such a client usually has in her role as client.

There seems to be a kind of imperialism implicit in these insight processes. As one gets further and further "into" a particular worldview, more and more of one's experienced universe becomes swept in, understood in terms of this view, and hence "explained." The pillars of a particular point of view come to seem more and more fundamental as pillars of explanation for larger and larger chunks of experience. As the reader is likely to have noticed, seeing the world in terms of point of view is not exempt from this process.

Actually, it is not quite accurate to say that the universe comes to "seem" largely explained or organized. The universe, or large parts of it, may actually *be* organized and explained by a particular point of view, if one takes this point of view. All sorts of things may really be real, but they each depend on an observer standing in the correct place in order to see them.

What is in error (from my point of view) is the idea that X that *seems* to be Y and is *actually* Z is therefore *not* Y. From a different point of view, inconsistent or not with the one that leads to Z, X may also really be Y. A chimney may really be a sexual symbol, but it also may really be a device for carrying away smoke and drawing oxygen through a fire. A therapy experience may be really beneficial in some terms and in others be really negative. In a couple I once saw, the wife was white and the husband black. She said of one of their acquaintances that he was a bit racially biased but that he was otherwise a decent person. The husband said of this acquaintance that he was otherwise a decent enough person but that he was racially biased. Even if there is only an inconsistency in the ordering of values, the difference between points of view can be quite sufficient, as in this last example, to be a focus of serious discontent.

Conflict arises regularly where it is imagined that only one point of view is correct or that all good people must hold a given point of view. The other side of this is that neither conflict nor much of anything else happens if no one asserts that such and such a point of view is where I stand, and acts accordingly. From where I stand, therefore, conflict is fed by a naive view of a singular reality and immobility is fed by sophistication that is not accompanied by a willingness to choose.

All of this may seem to lead to a serious dilemma. On one hand, conflict goes hand-in-hand with error. On the other, it is a likely consequence of the absolute necessity (with awareness or not—if one is actually to do anything) of choosing. Is conflict an unnecessary aggravation or is the possibility of conflict an essential consequence of getting anywhere? In present terms, this is not more of a dilemma than any of the other alternatives discussed here. It is a matter, in any given situation, of one's point of view. One must choose.

Where do the choices taken by this writer seem to lead? That is, given the view of therapy that has been described, including an emphasis on insight, candor, and respect, and a deemphasis of behavior, what if anything is one to do (in therapy) with respect to such interrelated issues as gender, expressiveness or restraint of sexuality, romance and practicality, economic systems, race and ethnicity? If I may say so myself, this is the wrong question. It is put in a way that seems to emphasize overt actions. Although it is clear that various activities have been praised or condemned in these pages, the overriding emphasis—in terms of therapy—is that what the clients overtly do, or what the therapist overtly does, is not of such great importance. The underlying purposes (thought out or otherwise), point of view, sensibility, caring and other feelings, are more crucial. These define what the therapist is "up to" in ways that cannot be spelled out by some list of strategies and techniques.

What I think I know at this point is that a respectful and caring search for expanded awareness about what clients are up to, attempting to stand back from trying to control their subsequent choices, is a good thing. I believe that all this is helpful to people while they are trying to become somehow more than they have been. What I have no way of knowing is what will become of these views as I learn more. I suspect that as I become more seeing of phenomena pointed out—in a sense created by—ideologies of our time, very much including those impinging immediately on intimate relationships, what I experience in the so-called consulting room will change and perhaps change greatly. I doubt that a tree-counter will notice much that is different, but I will, and the others in the room may also.

12

RESEARCH COMPUTATIONS

This section will start with the premise of a conventional data-collection process—administration of a questionnaire or coding of observed interaction—and sketch out a few possibilities for analysis. Actually carrying out these possibilities could require a fair amount of computation, but the ideas involved are fairly simple and require no unusual technical knowledge. Some of the possibilities mentioned here have been done before. For these there may be an issue of greater emphasis or degree. Other possibilities may be new, never done before. Maybe these new ideas are good ones, or maybe the reason they have never been done is because there are basic technical flaws that are overlooked here. On the other hand, if these ideas seem strange and new, they may do so partly because they come from different premises, from a line of thought relatively unconcerned with causality, discounting a one-to-one correspondence between particular discrete behaviors and particular inferences about their authors, and with more emphasis on contextuality and conditional inference.

The question at hand is, what would one do differently (either doing something new or doing more or less of something not new) if one were to accept the line of thought presented in this book? In research as in therapy, the fundamental answer is that what one does is less important than why it is done and how it is understood. The ideas that have been presented here do not require new procedures. Their implications are more along the lines of not doing some old and familiar things, such as experimental tests of causality, and permitting, as opposed to requiring, some new things.

The possibilities to be mentioned here are then offered as examples of things that might seem more plausible if one is interested in the description of people, their lives, and their attributes, and not in working under the shadow of a traditional and monolithic god of social science in which the received point of view is innocently and truly believed to be the only point of view or the only plausible point of view. In a way, there may be nothing more worth curious inquiry than an empirical, conceptual, or philosophical problem that is regarded as solved and settled.

There is a reason for speaking of possibilities rather than suggestions. The burden of this section is not to argue that these are good ideas for data analysis, although one or more of them might be. Rather, the point is to demonstrate that changing one's point of view can lead to substantial changes in procedure. The possibilities presented here are only examples presented to show that examples exist.

Several considerations went into deciding what to include in this section. First, the several ideas presented are all quantitative. They are all ways to manipulate numbers and lead to numbers that can be thought to describe individuals or groups. As such, they are intended to underline the fact that even such apparently cut-and-dried activities as run-of-the-mill data-analytic procedures spring from philosophical premises that might well be questioned every fifty years or so. Second, there is a deliberate attempt to jar the reader. If the reader cannot be budged from traditional thought at least her or his attention might be called to that thought being traditional rather than merely and obviously correct. Third, the procedures described are intended to be technically feasible. Commonly used procedures for analyzing questionnaire data, largely going back around fifty years, were once close to the limit of a social scientist's computing capacity. Now that almost everyone has easy access to a powerful mainframe computer and/or a personal computer, many more things are feasible. Indeed, I count on the popular fascination with Cuisinart data analysis as a source of interest in what follows. In the case of interaction analysis, conventional consideration of sequencing is already very heavily computational. So it seems desirable to include a possibility that is computationally less heavy.

Inferences from a Questionnaire

The most famous example of contextualized scoring of a questionnaire is surely the Minnesota Multiphasic Personality Inventory (Hathaway & McKinley, 1951). The inventors of this remarkable device decided that a person's score on some scales should depend on how the person did on other scales. They attempted to ascertain the person's propensity to lie and the person's propensity to fake bad. Other scale scores could then be adjusted to take such information into account. Most contextual efforts since then have been similar in that there has been a concern to remove or control for some factor that otherwise would spuriously affect a score.

Traditionally speaking, a given response to a questionnaire item contributes a fixed amount toward an individual's final score for some variable. There is a direct and concrete relationship between the response and the inference concerning the variable being measured. Controlling for some other measured variable may be regarded as attempting to correct for a weakness, in that the questionnaire is not as pure a measure of the desired variable as one might wish. This view is a bit limited. Why not imagine that the relationship between a group of measures and some inferred attribute is complex and conditional, and that no single measure can be identified as *the* measure of this attribute, no matter how purified? Discriminant function analysis, for example, goes somewhat in this direction by considering complex but not conditional relationships.

Finally, why not take this view at the item level rather than at the level of summed questionnaire scores? Basically in normal questionnaire scoring, each of a series of items generates a weight of some sort. Each item is considered separately and the weights are simply added together to form the total score. If conditional relationships among individual items are considered in deriving scores, the scoring procedure (1) comes closer to the intuitive idea that the proper interpretation of one assertion depends largely on its context of other assertions, (2) might provide the potential for whatever cross-checking is needed to reduce the impact of faking, confusion, and so on, and (3) enormously multiplies the information to be considered.

Even for a questionnaire of 30 items, astronomical sample sizes would be needed to study all possible combinations of item responses properly. However, it does not seem very wise to sacrifice all conditional information, including whatever there may be in a given sample, just because one would need the universe to study all imaginable conditional information. This is the present convention—studying no conditional information.

Consider a multi-item version of an item analysis. The goal is to find a scoring procedure for variable X, such that X will have a high correlation with variable Y. Dropping niceties, one might assign a scoring weight to each given response to an item. The assigned weight could be the mean value of Y, averaging over all instances of the given item response. For example, if five people answered True to item 1, and these five people had an average score of 3.2 on variable Y, then 3.2 would be the weight assigned to a response of True on item 1. In computing variable X, 3.2 would be added to a person's score if the person answered True on item 1. One could do this for each individual item in the pool being considered, and then one could do the same for each possible combination of two items. If there were only true-false items, each pair of two items would have four possible responses: TT, TF, FT, and FF. Each of these could then be assigned the appropriate mean value of Y. Hypothetically, the process could be repeated for each combination of three items, four items, five items, and so on. Resulting compound items, made up from one, two, three, four, or more original items, could then be treated in an almost conventional way. A given individual item would become part of a whole series of compound items, and one might not want the same individual item selected more than once. Some variance adjustments might be necessary. Compound items, however, could be evaluated and selected on the basis of (compound) item correlations with Y, or on the basis of (compound) item contributions to an overall correlation with Y, and added together to form a total scale, more or less in the ordinary way.

Now, if one computes the number of possible item-response combinations, determines how many observed instances of each response combination are needed for a useful estimate of its mean Y value, and multiplies these two numbers, one will immediately be in the astronomy business. A more modest way to proceed is to determine how many instances of a given response combination are needed and to study only those response combinations that occur with adequate frequency in a given sample. There is no need to settle for nothing just because everything is not likely to be available. A scoring system derived from some such computational process would no longer have built into it the necessity of one-to-one inference from an individual item response and some fixed inference (a fixed-scale weight).

Apart from the matter of one-to-one inference between an item response and a scale weight, scales traditionally are derived and then remain mostly fixed and inflexible. Even if generated by a process like the one just described, the questionnaire variable X is likely to be defined by a set of items and a known and mostly unchanging scoring system. Why? Is it possible that one aspect of the answer to this question has to do with mythology derived from the icon of operational definition? Perhaps a behavior-oriented mythology of one-to-one correspondence between behavior and inference, even if the inference is complex, has led us to reject out of hand the view that there are other possibilities.

Suppose the existence of a group of questionnaire items and a data set that includes responses to these items and information on other variables. It would be commonplace to regard some scoring system as a given and then to determine empirical relationships between the test score and the other variables. Alternatively, one could start without a scoring system and attempt to derive one from the data in hand. Certain relationships with the other variables would be taken as given, that is, as the relationships that the derived test score should have, and a scoring system could be developed that most closely fit these relationships.

So far, none of this is particularly exceptional. But note that there is not very much empirical content to the distinction between using relationships to determine questionnaire scoring and using question-naire scoring as a given in order to determine relationships. That is, you could not determine which of these was the more appropriate procedure by examining the numerical values in your data. In a sense, what is at issue here is in the mind of the researcher. If the researcher *decides,* perhaps on the basis of previous research that is found adequate, or perhaps largely on the basis of content validity, that a given scoring system is to define a test score, the researcher can then explore (further) how this score relates to other variables. If the researcher is convinced about how this score should relate to other variables, empirical findings that conflict with these views may be rejected. Instead of deciding that the relationships are other than they are supposed to be, the researcher may undo the previous decision about how the test score is to be defined, and think about changing the test. On the other hand, a researcher may approach an identical body of data with little in the way of preconcep-tions about test scoring. Perhaps there has been no previous research to establish a scoring system, or this researcher finds the previous work inadequate, or the researcher has been disabused of a previous decision about scoring on the basis of results such as those described above. This researcher then starts by *deciding* how the variable to be scored must relate to other variables. Rather than use a given scoring system to discover relationships, the researcher uses given relationships in order to discover the most appropriate scoring system.

In short, the distinction between using a scoring system to discover relationships, and using relationships to discover a scoring system, is a matter of point of view, of decisions or stands taken by the researcher.

Suppose one does not follow the ordinary sequence of test score derivation and then empirical determination of test correlates. Suppose instead one repeats the test derivation process over and over, with successive samples or successive kinds of samples. The consequence may be a number of similar but not identical scoring systems, one for each analysis. Yet (because of similar obtained fit to predecided relationships) each scoring system is thought to measure the same conceptual variable (for its appropriate sample). Our positivist hearts might groan at this thought, since how could different measurement procedures be thought to measure the same variable?

Here the answer is quite straightforward. Different measurement procedures are *not* being used. In each case, the measurement procedure is the same. Our problem, from this point of view, is that we have a narrow view of measurement procedure. It might not offend God to include item analyses in our concept of measurement procedure. Why should not the suit (the scoring system) be tailored to fit the individual customer (the particular group studied)?

It can be argued that following such a process would lead to wildly discrepant results from sample to sample and generally chaotic findings. Alternatively, it can be suggested that following such a process would only be a lot of work for little difference in results. Either of these is of course possible. I would only mention that what little replication now exists in social science suggests that chaos and discrepant findings are not strangers to us, and that the empirical consequences of doing something different will not be known until it is done.

Empirically discovered relationships between a test and other variables can be regarded as findings. As such, they have status and are thought of as accomplishment. What would a finding be if a defined pattern of relationships were taken as a given rather than as an empirical possibility? First, it should be added that findings of the sort just mentioned (of empirical relationships) are quite conditional. They depend on stands taken as to appropriate scoring systems (disregarding other necessary stands as not immediately pertinent). Where a stand is taken, things are fixed. Findings are in the areas not fixed, in effect where there are degrees of freedom. If there are no degrees of freedom, there are no findings. If there is no place where a stand is taken, as described here, the result is also that there are no findings. If there are shifts in where stands are taken, there are also shifts in where findings are possible.

Given the possibility sketched earlier, findings would be in terms of relationships beyond those predetermined and in terms of changes in scoring pattern. Also, what one would find, one hopes, might include a better idea of a given person's standing on some conceptual variable. It is possible that sometimes we might be most interested in learning something about our subjects, and in describing them as accurately as possible, and not so much interested in proving generalized abstractions about variables.

Supposing a primary interest in getting to the most accurate possible (quantitative) descriptions of the people being studied, there is still more mischief that can be done, except that it might not really be mischief. Suppose that at the conclusion of some process or other there is a matrix of correlations among a set of variables. Suppose further that, as earlier, the researcher takes a stand as to what the true correlations are, or should be, given accurate measurement. To simplify things, let the true correlations be perfect.

Now then, suppose that Fred Jones's scores on X are such that they average a certain amount greater than what would be predicted by his scores on all the other variables. Given the stand taken about relationships among variables, it appears that the score on X assigned to Fred is too high by this certain amount. Let us then lower his score to make it more accurate. An iterative procedure can be imagined that would make successive changes of this sort on each variable and for each observation. In effect, the process characterized as item analysis in the paragraphs above is continued by other methods. The process, that is, is not so much a matter of finding optimal items and item weights as it is a matter of finding the most accurate set of scores (given the conceptual specifications described earlier).

In one way of thinking, then, the key question is whether or not one is primarily getting at measurement values that are likely to be the most accurate (given a very well-developed conceptualization of the measured variable). For present purposes, however, it is more important to reemphasize that when point of view changes new possibilities become imaginable. The key question is thus the more general one: What is one's point of view, that is, what things does a researcher choose to take as given, so as to have a defined frame of reference from which to acquire findings in the areas not taken as given? A more traditional point of view, and the point of view informing the earlier discussion, are themselves only possible points of view. There may be any number of others.

Sequence Analysis

One way to make plausible the detailed study of human interaction is a predisposition to believe that interaction is largely reducible to a series of discrete acts and that earlier acts cause later ones. It is possible that this predisposition to reductionist causality has had a central influence on the study of human interaction sequences. Whether this speculation is actually supportable or not, it will be used here as a kind of rhetorical stance that may highlight two or three details in the study of sequences and may highlight as well some possibilities for doing things differently.

Of course, I really do believe that a propensity to accept reductionist causality has had a major influence. It is otherwise difficult to make sense of efforts to discover *which* bits of interaction cause each other or the apparent interest in teaching therapists to enact the therapist side of sequences that have sometimes seemed to have happy outcomes. However, this belief is not essential to what follows. In the present context it is only a position taken as a way to organize the computational suggestions.

Consider the view that various coded events are both the causes of later events and the results of earlier ones. Earlier events push later ones into existence, so to speak. Thus, conditional probabilities may be computed, indicating that if X happens, there is then a certain probability that Y will follow. This way of looking seems quite natural.

Suppose however that a view is adopted in which later events draw earlier ones into existence? A simple not to say innocent view of Newtonian mechanics might make this possibility seem a bit farfetched, but after all it is really quite common to think of people as having intentions and hence acting for all the world as if some goal is drawing them to it. Perhaps this shift in worldview, as it were, might jog one's imagination sufficiently to suggest computing conditional probabilities in the backwards direction. That is, when X happens, what is the probability that it was preceded by Y?

Observations are made of a violent married couple. They always greet each other with a cheery hello, but within a surprisingly short time they turn to hitting each other. The actions of this couple are coded, conditional probabilities are computed, and probabilistic trees are generated showing various branching pathways of possible action sequences. Which is more interesting, the various pathways that are likely to be started by "hello" or the various (backward-running) pathways that all end up in violence? The distinction may be related fairly directly to the conceptual distinction between emphasizing violence as caused by some system properties literally going out of control—the substrate view—and emphasizing violence as being itself an intended activity with important functions in the interactive system.

Conditional probabilities also seem to be consonant with another aspect of underlying conceptualization, namely, that causes are proximal. Classically speaking, one looks at the probabilistic influence of one event on the next event. There seem to be mixed feelings about this aspect of conceptualization as evidenced by the use of various lags. Conditional probabilities are computed referring to the probability of Y happening as the next event after X (a lag of one), the next event after that (a lag of two), the next event after that (a lag of three), and so on. An entire set of conditional probabilities might be computed for each of a substantial number of such lags, generating the considerable task of making sense of a great many computations.

Using a selection of lags is an attempt to escape from being limited to immediately proximal sequelae, but the escape is not complete. In the first place, there is not a clear and straightforward way to integrate the massive data derived from doing a series of differently lagged analyses. In the second place, if a series of events follow each other in an orderly way, but with a varying number of other, intervening events, the orderly sequence may escape notice. In the third place, as the lag value goes up, the number of intervening events skipped over goes up, and it can be assumed that differences among these patterns of skipped events have a progressively greater influence on sequelae. The upshot of all this is that conditional probabilities may work well for immediately proximal sequelae, but are probably less and less revealing as the lag value grows.

The relative unsuitability of conditional probabilities for other than immediately proximal relationships is not their only shortcoming. The fact that each coefficient refers only to two points in time means that implications for sequences longer than two time points are drawn only laboriously and to some extent indirectly.

What the use of conditional probabilities does is preserve absolutely the before-and-after relationship of any two coded events (that happen to be separated by the exact lag value being used). This is certainly important if the question of what causes what, among coded events, is important. It also emphasizes the view that one discrete act can be treated sensibly as if it were the consequence of one other discrete act.

Suppose, however, that the focus on reductionist causality can be relaxed a bit, including some relaxation of the focus on immediately proximal relationships. Perhaps it is possible to look at sequences in such a way as to identify similar or repetitive sequences, of somewhat longer lengths than just two events. Similarity can refer to the tendency of the same coded events to turn up in more or less (not necessarily exactly) the same places in different sequences. What is likely to be lost is the information that event X, say, *always* precedes (or follows) event Y. That is, similarity of location may not refer to a before or after relationship.

Let us pursue this idea of similarity of sequential patterns without emphasis on exactly what comes before what. A data set to be analyzed, characterizing one sequence of events, would consist of, say, ones and zeros (happenings and not-happenings), organized by some list of codes (events that happen or do not), and by some list of times (time 1, time 2, and so on). If a series of sequences were included in the data, the ones and zeros would also be organized by a list of sequences. In effect, then, the data would form a three-dimensional solid of codes by times by sequences.

There are several ways to collapse this solid into a two-dimensional space.

(1) Each row can be a sequence, and each column can be a code category. Cell entries would be time values, that is, the times that a given code occurred in a given sequence. Thus this would be one way to summarize a list of sequences. Each line (row) would be one sequence showing the time(s) at which particular coded events occurred.

(2) Each row can again be a sequence but now with each column being a time. Cell entries would be the codes that occurred at particular times in these sequences. This would be another way to summarize a list of sequences, one summary per row. Reading from left to right (assuming the columns are ordered this way), one would read a list of coded events in the order they occurred.

(3) Summing over sequences, the result is a matrix of times by codes. Cell entries would be lists of sequences indicating for which sequences a particular code happened at a particular time. In this case, the results do not so clearly seem to be summaries of sequences, although all the data may be preserved in this form. On the other hand, when the data set is presented this way, the cell entries (lists of sequences) provide some direct information about similarity among sequences. Sequences in which the

same codes occur at the same times might, that is, be thought of as similar.

Type 1 has an analytic advantage over the other two types by virtue of what is entered in the cells. That is, cell entries—by definition—are measures on a common continuum (time) and subject to mathematical operations that may not be appropriate for cell entries in the other two types of summary. Cell entries in summary Types 2 and 3 may be only nominal designations.

A cluster analysis of rows might be used with a Type 1 matrix to determine groups of similar sequences or some other kind of analysis might be used to reach similar results. That is, this way of dealing with sequences of coded activities leads directly to ways that similarities and differences among sequences can be described and repetitious patterns of interaction identified. Clustering columns might also be used as a route to defining functionally equivalent codes, that is, codes that tend to occur at about the same time.

Assuming that no inferential statistics are used (as such), all of the above could be applied to an individual case, that is, to one independent observation, and cases compared as to the different kinds of sequence clusters they generate.

These analyses would not burn up data quite as voraciously as some conditional probability work, and might more reasonably be referred to as data *reduction*. To be exact, a full correlational analysis of S sequences and C codes would mean computing $(S(S-1))/2$ or $(C(C-1))/2$ coefficients, whereas a full conditional probability analysis could involve $C**2$ coefficients, times the number of lags to be studied.

Most important, this form of analysis would have a chance of discovering sequential relationships that are fairly dependable but that occur over varying amounts of time (and hence might not show up in any fixed time interval analysis of conditional probabilities). Putting this another way, it provides the possibility of discovering sequential relationships among a series of codes (not limited to two codes at a time), even though the codes involved may be separated from each other by varying amounts of irrelevant material.

From the point of view of reductionist causality, the sort of analysis described here has serious shortcomings. It does not indicate whether or not X is regularly followed by Y, only whether or not X and Y tend to occur at similar (or different) places in a collection of sequences.

There is no intention here to suggest a way of working that should replace the use of conditional probability, and similar measures. The intended suggestion is only that some other variations are possible and perhaps plausible. If empirical research is to be meaningful to those with a variety of underlying conceptual frameworks, the development of new ways to see data analysis (not just more complicated procedures for implementing old ways) may be significant work that should be supported.

13

THE FUTURE OF IMAGINATION

Mark Twain said that the world is divided into two kinds of people, those who divide the world into two kinds of people, and those who do not. Thus we plunge into one more discussion of a conceptual polarity but this time a polarity that is recursive. The assertion of the polarity is itself a position within the polarity.

Physics before this century has been supplanted by a newer physics, courtesy of Albert Einstein and many other people who imagined a worldview very much more complex than that of Newtonian physics. Thus this worldview is different than that of Newtonian physics. Yet, Newtonian mechanics is contained within this more contemporary view. The physics that is the historical child is the logical parent, that is, the earlier view is a special case of the later view. It might be imagined that from the point of view of an unconverted Newtonian, the more modern physics would be thought simply wrong, or crazy. However, from the modern view, Newton is easily comprehensible, and—properly circumscribed—correct.

Does psychotherapy work? If one takes the view that there really is such a thing as mental (or family) health, and the view that therapy is something that can be administered like aspirin, this question might have an answer. If one takes a view of therapy as a complex human relationship with many ways in which it can be viewed, and many ways its meanderings can be evaluated, the question just might not have an answer. The question might even be absurd, except for one fact. To imagine the large number of ways in which therapy can be construed includes imagining some in which the question posed above does have a clear and well-defined answer.

Let us then ask a meta-question. Is the question, "Does psychotherapy work?" a meaningful one? There are two likely answers. One is that this is a clear and meaningful question, perhaps even an empirical one, and an important question to answer. The other is that in many ways it depends on what one means. With some interpretations of the question and its terms it is meaningful, and with others it is not. Those who provide the former answer (absolutely yes) are likely not to understand the latter one or to agree with it. However, those who provide the latter answer can easily understand those with the former answer and may even—with some reservations—agree with them.

Consider civil liberties. A person of liberal views believes that all persons should have the right to say what they please. A person of less liberal views believes that some opinions should be silenced, including the view that all people should be able to say what they please. The former person has no problem with the existence of the latter individual, and the latter person's expression of opinion, but the reverse is not true.

Putting this contrast in more general terms, we can imagine someone who might be called a conceptual fundamentalist, a person who believes that there is one correct way to see the world. Other ways are obviously wrong. With somewhat more imagination, another individual might find a number of different ways to see the world, perhaps even including the way just referred to as fundamentalist. However, if any one of us is able to imagine the existence of both of these persons, and that each makes some kind of sense, then a position has been taken in the second camp. Imagining that fundamentalism is only one way to see the world is already leaving fundamentalism behind.

This is a serious problem in conceptual discussion. In considering alternative ways to see our work, there is not likely to be the joining of a substantive issue with those who do not see alternative views. There is not likely to be a debate as to whether one set of views is correct and the other not, or as to which view is preferable. More likely, received wisdom is thought of as reality, and more relativist views are thought of as either trivially true or confused foolishness. Once a more relativist view is understood, it wins automatically. There is no way to imagine the existence of alternative ways of seeing and at the same time to believe that there is only one way. Before understanding arrives, however, if it ever does, what seems superficially to be a conceptual discussion feels more like one side speaking to the deaf and the other side patiently tolerating the befuddled.

In an ideal world, so to speak, such a problem would be serious but not grave. Those who thought alike could work together, communicate with each other, and simply get by without having everyone around believe that the work was justified. Academic freedom is supposed to make this kind of thing possible, is it not?

The trouble is that in our less-than-perfect world, those who are more enamored of simple worldviews are the decisive, action-oriented people who by and large control the mechanisms that support (or not) the work that is done and reward it (or do not). They are likely to be highly visible proponents of technique-oriented work because techniques are easy to describe and sound like something real. They certainly sound more real than the hemming and hawing of those whose worldviews are so relativistic that there seems to be no place to set down one's feet.

Thus there is a two-sided problem. Those with a conservative view are not likely to leap to the support of fuzzy sounding, downright strange-sounding views. And those with the imagination to see a huge range of possibilities may lack whatever it takes (courage?) to plant their feet in one place or another, to take a stand with the full knowledge that another stand, many other stands, could also have been taken. Given the willingness to take stands, however, and to give up dead ends inherited from the past, almost anything may be possible. Perhaps even the dead ends, once truly abandoned, might return with new life. It is once again the happy story of successful romance with its surrender that permits rebirth.

Imagination creates our worlds. Once created, they may have a power that is easily thought to be far from imaginary. I have argued elsewhere (Ryder, 1972) that power, real life, political power, is largely a matter of imagination. Gandhi imagined, dreamed up, the view that powerlessness itself could be a political weapon of great force, and it was true. Martin Luther King, Jr., applied that weapon in the American scene with consequences that few would have thought possible.

Japan had an advantage at the start of World War II in having realized that we would sell them scrap metal that they could later shoot back at us. Our failure of imagination was expensive. Confusion, weakness, and bad chains of communication have all been turned to advantage in guerrilla wars of the "weak" against the strong. How do you beat an enemy that has no chain of command and no organized system to disrupt?

The spying game in World War II, as described by Goffman (1962), was serious, with many lives thought to be at stake. Yet it consisted largely of intellectually sophisticated hairsplittings in which not just the strategies followed, but any judgment as to which side gained by a given event was a subjective judgment. In a sense, the entire game was largely a matter of competing imaginations, including the scorekeeping.

All I am trying to get across here is that when saying imagination is powerful, there need be no quotation marks on "powerful." The power involved can be quite real.

Family therapists around the country often seem to imagine their programs as being of low status in their home institutions, and losers when resources are low. Why is this? Focusing only on the therapists themselves, why can they not create for themselves a better situation? I would say, of course they can. First, it must be imagined. Perhaps many of us in the family business were the children who felt that we came in second in our own families. Later, we go into a profession that seems to promise ways we can triumph over family evils, whether the families fight us or not. Leaping eagerly for final success, we forget that we will inevitably follow our own path whether or not it is the path we claim to want, and discover that in a slightly different way we have become, once more, the disadvantaged child. If we live through events that somehow have us imagining, really seeing, the realistic possibility of another scenario, the other scenario does become a realistic possibility.

Naturally, this generalization about family therapy is just fantasy and has no claim to factuality. The truth of it is the therapeutic truth that few of us imagine as a realistic possibility a world, a profession, a life, that is dramatically better than what we have. Imagining such a thing is common, but few of us imagine it to be a realistic possibility that individuals or groups of people can actually do, might actually do, will actually do.

Sometimes it even seems that those who appear to fight most hard for change of some sort are kept active by frustration, not by success. With success, anger diminishes, energy diminishes, and the fight wanes. It becomes necessary to redefine apparent success as minimal or even as failure, to keep alive a fight that by its nature can never be successful. There may even be some question as to whether the point of the anger is to maintain the fight or whether the point of the fight is to maintain the anger.

So much for modesty. Adequate imagination to see possibilities where futility might well be seen, imagination to notice assumptive givens and to question them, imagination that provides a new way of seeing one's world, and watching black and white turn to technicolor before your eyes, all this is transformation with consequences far beyond the imaginary. One can call imagination of this sort insight, and so it is. It goes beyond heightened awareness of what is, to heightened awareness of what is not yet, but is realistic and possible; beyond what is, but not far beyond.

Once one really accepts—sees, directly perceives—something as a realistic possibility, it is immediately, in the present tense, just that—a realistic possibility. What was nonexistent in one's personal universe a moment ago, is now present and seen to have been present perhaps always. Again, there is a difference between toying with an idea and knowing it as something that actually can be made real. The former may be only one more declaration of despair, as, "It could be, but it probably will not be. In the end, things will not work." In the latter, mulling and processing are replaced by the turning of wheels to make it happen.

Amazingly, imagination seems to have gotten a bad name in social science and therapy. It seems associated with fuzzy-minded idealism, impractical policies, and indecision. If there are many ways to see the world and to deal with it, and many complications, the result may be immobilizing, but it need not be. In the same way, curiosity seems to have gotten short shrift in social science and therapy, with the pragmatic interest in fixing things seen as somehow more scientific. What else can science be, if not the organized and systematic pursuit of curiosity?

Imagination can make things happen. When I first came to my present university position, my school had a traditional laboratory nursery school that had two hour sessions per day for children aged 3 to 4. I wanted to open a full day-care center. Two months before my arrival, the Board of Trustees had decided there should be no day-care center. We therefore simply maintained our traditional Child Development Laboratory. We also expanded the hours from two to eight per day and expanded the age range so that now we accepted children as young as 6 weeks and as old as 8 years.

There was no doctoral program in my school. The university was refusing to support any new programs and was even asking schools to reduce the number of doctoral programs they had at present. We went to such a school and offered to take one of their programs off their hands. They agreed.

Ultimately, we all die. In the meantime, we do not have to lose nearly as often or as heavily as we sometimes seem to think. We might wish to excuse our failures and losses by repeatedly showing them to be inevitable, but probably they are not.

Anyway, avoiding loss is not necessarily the main thing. A stockbroker once lectured me severely for being too cautious in an investment. The point of investment, he said, is not, repeat not, to avoid losing money.

   Those caught up in fundamentalist beliefs about science, or about human lives and relationships, may or may not come to see that their views create their own proofs, and that other views may also be made real; but once seen it is a self-evident truth. To an extent that is far from imaginary, and whether or not any of us sees it clearly, there is a far better existence waiting out there, in our personal lives and in our professions, waiting only to be imagined as a realistic possibility, and seized.

14

TOWARD MORE CARE AND MODESTY

Socially oriented therapy is one way for change to occur in particular parties—individuals, families, couples, and perhaps other groupings as well. But suppose one would like to see change (obviously I would) in a whole collection of disciplines, or maybe just in one discipline, or even in one subdiscipline. How about just a piece of one subdiscipline?

This group of essays as a whole is of course one way of attempting to influence disciplinary change. It has attempted to persuade the reader that all is not well in some areas of social science and socially oriented therapy. If success means something like knowing a lot more about a subject matter (referring more to people than to variables), or being much more able to "fix" social ills, unequivocal success has eluded this group of disciplines, or at least so it has been argued.

The argument has gone on to urge in a number of ways that if we reach for less, we might accomplish more. Greater modesty and care, it has been urged, are in our interest. Modesty has been implied in a number of different senses. First, it has been suggested that one must, in effect, choose among different ways of regarding people and their activities. There just are no right answers to some "point of view" questions, and anyway, one must take some position. The immodest if not arrogant idea that anyone can know what "real" reality is, independent of point of view, has been taken to task, including the idea that one can somehow escape from taking any position on these issues.

Several examples relating to point of view have been discussed. Some people who disagree with the examples provided here would probably be able to come up with other examples that support the same general conclusion.

Second, it has been suggested that some apparently desirable objectives might best be set aside. Demonstrations of causality, exclusive attention to objective behavior, and freedom from values have been noted as goals that might largely be beyond our grasp and/or more harmful than helpful. It has even been suggested that great efforts at reaching some of these goals might have opposite effects to the ones seemingly intended.

Third, it has been suggested that overselling occurs and may have occurred in the past. General societal support for our work has been eroded in part, it has been argued, by excessive claims.

These urgings for greater modesty have had a paradoxical aspect in the implicit idea that professionals might more often stand up and be counted, that is, take positions that are acknowledged to be personal ones and not totally dictated by "the facts." Arguments have been made repeatedly against the idea that there is one correct point of view, or one correct paradigm, and against the idea that the personal stands of an observer are only inconvenient obstacles in the pursuit of "actual" reality. In effect, attention has been called to the false belief, as seen here, that all meaningful questions have one most correct answer. It has been implied that this belief serves at least one questionable purpose. Namely, it is a way for professionals to avoid taking personal responsibility for positions they may hold as people.

Thus the essay on minimal therapy loops back on the others in its consideration of responsibility. Building on some of the conceptual points made earlier, it emphasizes among other things the importance of accepting responsibility and the view that being more aware of one's personal role in one's life is a significant kind of growth. What is meant here by looping back is that this last statement is applicable not only to clients but also to the professionals who serve them and who do research. It is a capsule commentary on much that is in the earlier essays.

Perhaps there is a sense in which some social science and substrate-oriented social therapy constitute a large-scale effort to avoid existential responsibilities of choosing, of taking positions. "Empirical facts" as dictators of one's views are ever so much easier on one than knowing that one cannot know but must decide anyway. To mention once again Roszak's (1972) citation of Blake, science may be partly an *effort* to see the world through "dead men's eyes." To push the metaphor a bit, success at such an endeavor may make functioning as a professional easier but also less alive.

Therefore, there is still another way to express the suggestion for more modesty. It is that we forego attempts to leave behind inescapable "weaknesses" of the human condition in trying to become more (or mere) efficient devices in the service of impersonal science. Permission to ourselves and to each other, to relax, to allow ourselves our unavoidable shortcomings, and to do so in public, may be a more productive path in the long run. Once this path has freed the imagination, modesty has served its purpose and has led to a result that may be far from modest. The metaphor of successful romance is used to characterize this process of surrender and new freedom.

If we are to understand people, or approach scientific or clinical objectives as construed in some other way, it might be better to be more concerned about what seems helpful, or what does not, than about rules and regulations that prescribe how to be, say, a proper scientist. When aspects of research technique are urged because they seem to serve certain ends, and then develop into ends themselves, the original goals may not be well served. For example, there is no guarantee that information expressed numerically is more enlightening than information in prose. If information is to be numerical, there is no guarantee that more statistical processing leads to more enlightenment. The Cuisinart approach may have its place in research as in cooking, but blind overuse can just blur the flavors of the original data.

The paradoxical suggestion that the acknowledgement of not knowing be accompanied by a willingness to take stands anyway is one that this collection of essays has attempted to follow. Modesty has been urged, but with the immodest implication that the stands taken here might be worth taking seriously. If this is self-contradictory, the contradiction is about to become more glaring in the present essay. It is going to suggest disciplinary change intended to make modesty and care, along with some other things, more feasible. As might be seen even in the preceding sentence, this essay will treat social systems largely as substrate with the implicit view that actions by a few (intentional) people might have noticeable effects of some significance.

Another mixed message in these essays is along a dimension of difficulty and effort. One way to read this message is as a recommendation for more thought, more care, more caution, more attention to epistemology and to axiology, and more attention to the ultimate purposes of one's work, assuming that the chief purpose is a vague thing called understanding.

Choosing pathways easily, because "research shows" the correct way, or making moral decisions readily because right and wrong seem obvious or seem to be matters of descriptive fact, these may be doing too easily what should be done only with difficulty.

Yet there is also a message here to ease off, to relax, to give up on impossible goals, and to stroll rather than run through the difficult tasks that we may have assigned ourselves.

These two messages are intimately related to each other. Narrow and absolutist restrictions make life easier by reducing decision making and make life harder by telling one not to wander at all off the straight and narrow (and perhaps frustrating and painful) path. Relativism has the opposite implications.

There is even another apparent contradiction within the message to ease off on moralistic restrictions, since minimal therapy is virtually defined by restrictions, many of which are rooted in value judgments. Yes, but. One "but" is that these are value judgments labeled as such, at least for the most part. Those with different values will, no doubt, feel free to disregard them. The other "but" is that the restrictive aspects of minimal therapy are primarily intended to avoid imposing restrictive value judgments on the life choices of clients and to avoid teaching them, as they have probably been taught many times already, that their personal freedom to choose and manage their own lives is severely restricted.

To put it simply, in the therapy described here therapists restrict themselves from restricting others' choices and awareness of choice. This is the not very original idea that one person's freedom might well stop when it begins to hamper another person's freedom.

This brings up another mixed message, or perhaps it is just a 45-degree twist on the question of difficulty or ease. One message is that the number of choices available is really substantial. Since correct answers are not to be found for many point-of-view questions, people might (the message might even be read as "should") feel free to take a wide variety of positions and work accordingly.

Alternatively, the implication has been made that certain aspects of professional work have been wrong here or there and should be improved. Yes, it is true that I have ideas about fine work and poor work and will reward one and not the other if possible. This comes back to the starting place of the present discussion. To say that one might well be modest about what can be known is not to say that one should (according to my values) abdicate taking positions. What is important is that positions taken that are fundamentally matters of value do not masquerade as empirical facts and that positions are not taken in such a way as to prevent dissenting views from being heard.

A few years ago I was third author of a paper (Doherty, McCabe, & Ryder, 1978) criticizing a particular modality for helping people improve their marriages. There were a number of things we did not like about Marriage Encounter. Speaking now only for myself, it was obvious that this large movement had developed many variations and that almost anything said about it was only sometimes true. It seemed obvious as well that many people felt their lives to have been improved by Marriage Encounter (whereas some people felt the opposite was true). I was not very happy with the value system regarding marriage that usually seemed to be expressed in Marriage Encounter, but what the hell? They have a right to their point of view. I was a lot less happy with the way that value system was urged on people, since it seemed manipulative and unfair. What was (and is) really unforgivable was the attitude sometimes expressed explicitly that Marriage Encounter had a direct line to God. The value system of Marriage Encounter was described as God's point of view, with no room for any disagreement to be regarded with respect. Saint Paul, for example, might have raised an eyebrow at this dismissal of his less enthusiastic attitude toward marriage.

Apart from the intrinsically personal and subjective aspects of attaching values to things, almost any serious evaluation in social science or clinical work has also a subjective aspect in identifying that which is valued. To insist that the entities to which value is attached be reduced to objectifiable perhaps countable things that can be identified unambiguously is to invite crass and superficial judgment. The consequences of a reward system based on such judgments may not be what was initially desired.

Consider green peas. People used to buy peas that were a nice shade of green because that seemed to be a way to get better peas. The "pea merchants," as it were, were reinforced for selling better peas. One consequence, probably not desired by the average consumer, was that peas came to be dyed a nice, even, luminescent shade of green. Some meat too, at least hamburger, has come to have a gorgeous red surface in some markets under which the undoctored meat is drably brown.

It would be nice if public schools actually educated people. One way to push them in that direction might be to make sanctions (for teachers or schools) contingent on students' academic progress as measured by grades, numbers of students promoted, or standardized tests. Rumor has it that such efforts can lead to higher grades, more students promoted, and sometimes even higher test scores (if students are effectively coached or easier tests are found) but without necessarily a substantial change in how much learning goes on.

When objectifiable criteria are identified for excellence that is fundamentally something more subtle, it can be expected with some confidence that an effective reward system will have more effect on the criteria than on the excellence. In effect, the criteria will lose some of the validity they might once have had.

Faculty member A writes 6 or 7 scholarly papers and is awarded tenure. Faculty member B publishes 30 papers and is denied tenure. The justification for this distinction is said to be that A's papers are brilliant, masterful, fascinating, whereas B's are pedestrian, dull, redundant, and ultimately trivial as a group.

In my opinion (speaking as an administrator), an administrator who makes such a decision based on such an argument might be asking for Big Trouble. Contradicting a superficial piece of evidence such as paper counting with a more careful—but subjective—evaluation is possible surely, but is not as easy, and (hence) is not as common as it might be.

When B's lawyer arrives, it will become abundantly clear that (1) the values held by this administrator are not universally shared, and (2) subjective judgment is unfair, since it does not provide unambiguous guidelines about what to do in order to acquire tenure. Furthermore, subjectivity provides an administrator with the opportunity for expressing personal antagonism that may have nothing to do with B's work and by the same token provides B with the opportunity to charge that the negative evaluation is due to personal antagonism.

This anecdote is exaggerated, of course, but also has more than a little truth in it. The same situation seems to apply to credentials provided by professional organizations. That is, standards that have the broadest possible acceptance, translated into criteria that are maximally objective, are the safest way to go.

In short, values that are not universally shared, and subjectivity in the implementation of values, can lead to unfairness and to the appearance of unfairness along with much discomfort to those evaluated and to those doing the evaluating. Reducing standards to those that are almost universally held, and to objective criteria, can lead to mediocrity.

There are two notable examples of subjective evaluation, or something like it, that seem to be thriving in our field and hence that might deserve some attention. Journal evaluations of scholarly work are notoriously subjective and often unfair. Yet the evaluation process appears to continue relatively unaffected by protests from disgruntled authors. Perhaps one reason for the relative success of this process is that a rejected author usually can go to another journal and try again. Perhaps the existence of journals (or advisory editors) with a variety of different standards helps to make possible the unthreatened (and relatively unthreatening) existence of a given journal or advisory editor with relatively unique standards.

The other example is of clinicians who regularly discuss their work with each other and who seem calm about acknowledging personal feelings and other attributes that make them uncomfortable and that hinder clinical work. Such people seem to have learned an ethic that acknowledging weakness is a strength. They do not destroy each other for revealing foibles but rather compliment each other and respect each other for their bravery and honesty.

Assuming an interest in professional modesty, and a belief that the best criticism is partly subjective and based on standards that may not be generally shared, it might be useful to consider ways to expand and build on the strengths of these two examples.

The moral of the journal example may be that the existence of alternative evaluative processes, or some other way to reduce the cost of receiving a negative judgment, is a way to save an evaluation system from being pushed to the level of some objective lowest common denominator.

It is also true of journal rejections that they happen to virtually everyone, which brings us to the second example. When comments that might not feel very good are a part of everyone's experience, they hurt less. There is also something more subtle about the clinical process described. There seems to be an ethic among some clinicians that makes self-criticism (or something very like it) not only palatable but a positive aspect of self-esteem.

I do not presume to know how to foster the growth of such an ethic, except perhaps to urge it, but urge it I do. I would like to see this ethic become dominant among researchers and more extended among clinicians. There is something preferable in scholarly presentations that include some self-criticism or in papers that seem to take an actual interest in pointing to their own weaknesses. Those clinical presentations that make the clinical process seem like a smoothly functioning machine begin to develop a dubious aroma quite quickly. Perhaps it might help if editors and those who run meetings can be persuaded to prefer work with a few visible blemishes to the scholarly counterpart of peas that are implausibly green.

Regular insistence on self-criticism in a paper might well be required by editors. Advisory editors then would have to evaluate the quality of the self-criticism along with the quality of the rest of the paper to keep this policy from becoming an empty formality. Another possibility to be tried might be to accompany each published paper with a brief published critique, not by the author. The expense in journal space might be amply repaid in terms of greater usefulness to the serious reader and in terms of the self-restraint to be expected from people who know that criticism is inevitable.

All sorts of ways can be imagined to reduce the cost of negative evaluation. The existence of alternative journals may be, as suggested above, one way that is currently in place. Another might be to facilitate greater variety among professional positions and roles. If a person could go readily to a different and (for this person) more suitable institution, or to a different role within an institution, negative evaluation might have a less fatal effect. The present tenure system might be quite counterproductive in these terms, since it often seems to demand that a person be excellent at all the roles anyone in academia is to fulfill—teaching, scholarship, and service—or be out of a job and virtually unemployable. Even the safety achieved when tenure is acquired can increase the pressure on junior faculty, since nonproductive senior people can lead administrators to lean more on those who can be leaned on.

Tenure once acquired allows the freedom to work relatively free of career-threatening sanctions, or at least that is what is supposed to happen. The existence of radically nonproductive tenured people (or am I only imagining this?) suggests that some greater sanctions might need be devised for them if only for the morale of junior people.

Clinical credentialing is a very serious matter both in terms of the quality of services to be delivered and in terms of the potential costs to people denied credentials. It is not easy to see a way that the cost of a negative evaluation could be substantially reduced here without increasing costs in terms of service delivery. However, there may be little to prevent the growth of supplementary credentialing that would not be essential for professional employment.

Perhaps there could be some kind (or multiple kinds) of senior credentials based on careful and subjective evaluation that would be desirable to have in addition to an actual or de facto license to practice. Were this kind of credentialing to be more popular than it is now, there might be less reason to worry about a lowest common denominator quality of some baseline credentialing. In passing, it might be really unfortunate if senior credentialing developed that leaned heavily on counting such things as numbers of clients seen, years of experience, numbers of workshops attended, or weight of scholarly publications.

Thus, in this fantasy of the future, more subjective evaluations might exist but with consequences tamed to civilized proportions. Almost everyone would be stung, at least now and then, but few with fatal consequences. To wax religious, sort of, more would be chilled but fewer frozen.

All this talk of evaluations has said little about how evaluations are supposed to work or why. One obvious possibility is that an individual develops into a better clinician, a more careful and thoughtful scholar, or improves in another way, as a consequence of some sequence of rewards and nonrewards based on evaluations. Another way evaluations work is to facilitate selection among persons with only secondary concern about changing their performance. A series of traffic tickets may be intended to improve a driver's performance, but a license revocation is intended to improve driving performance in general by eliminating someone from the low end of the distribution.

In addition to problems affecting evaluations in general, evaluations for selection can be at the mercy of an available selection ratio. To be more exact, if the number of persons selected is to be kept up to some level, the selection ratio is at the mercy of how many persons are available to be evaluated. Perhaps some more absolute attitude to selection, until available places are filled, is more important than either a selection ratio or a guarantee that selected numbers remain sufficiently large.

Biggest is not necessarily best, nor is it even likely to be best if size is achieved by an accepting attitude to work that is not quite good. I would like to see fewer students trained, fewer professionals devoted to (less but better) scholarly work, and professional meetings that do not find it necessary to swell their ranks by accepting as many papers for presentation as is humanly possible.

It may be unfortunate that academic viability has some relationship to numbers of undergraduates taught, but it is a situation that can probably be survived. If the same relationship applies to numbers of graduate students, excellence in graduate training may not survive, much less grow.

Surely, no graduate education in large numbers can replace the one-on-one close relationship between a senior person and an apprentice. At some point every field needs nothing less than brilliant work. Brilliance is not mass produced. It is not produced at all, in fact. If anything, it is carefully selected, individually nurtured, and allowed ultimately to go its own way.

Just considering the care and intensity required by the best graduate education, smaller is better. There is even more reason for thinking small if one looks ahead at the numbers of prospective scholars a field can absorb well. At least in some areas, far more people are being trained than the scholarly enterprise is—or perhaps should be—prepared to accept. Apart from the human cost to those forced out of the system, the great pressure to seem like a producer in order to get a job may not bode well for the success of a selection process that tries, presumably, to recruit people with strong intrinsic motivation.

It would be nice to see the number of active scholars reduced to those who are strongly motivated to increase human understanding in some way and who may have some slight talent at it. Harking back to the earlier discussion of providing alternatives, this means, at a minimum, that people who are not strongly motivated to scholarship must have other ways to survive professionally and even to thrive. It would even be nice to see the remaining scholars write fewer papers. Fewer but better.

Scholarship as a whole might benefit from such a pruning operation. There might be a smaller and richer literature, and hence there might be less noise in the system. There might be less need to compete with persons who mostly want professional advancement without necessarily being strongly motivated to acquire greater understanding of some subject matter and who might be heavily involved in "selling" their work. Honest modesty about the fruits of a study is likely to suffer in a competition with people who require immodesty for their survival. It is possible that a less competitive atmosphere might be engendered among the remaining scholars. Finally, any improvement in the perceived average quality of published work would seem bound to improve the morale of those who would like to build on the work of others.

Yes, there is a certain paradoxical quality to urging cautious and thoughtful work, and a permissive attitude to varying points of view, and then urging systemic changes that seem particularly suited to one set of views. However, it may be naive to assume that we can each take Voltaire's advice to cultivate our own gardens and that an attitude of live and let live will be emulated by others. If the professional work we do is really important to us, it might be important to take whatever steps are needed to see that we, and others, are permitted to do it in a thoughtful and careful way. The most serious matter is that right now there is low survival value for a thoughtful junior person who does modest work without a production line or sales mentality.

Direct efforts at shaping research and clinical work exist at present and on a substantial scale. From a systemic point of view, live and let live may not be an available option.

Every agency with money for research support attempts to provide support for "better" work and to discourage "worse" work. Federal agencies generate priority lists for the topics they want studied, which means that a strong influence is provided on what topics actually are studied. It is doubtful that the current fascination with behavioral medicine is only a logical outgrowth of developments within psychology. More likely it has resulted from the perceived availability of new "markets" for services.

The recent years of continuing professional education are another example of an idea reaching the point of exerting influence, even coercion, on professionals who may or may not feel the need of it. This particular change effort is an example of "behavioral" influence that may show some of the limitations to changes that only affect fairly crass behavior. People may be required to attend workshops but cannot be required to learn much. Some of the people giving workshops may be motivated to provide events that are interesting and trendy, but not too demanding. Workshops have become big business, and I may not be alone in groaning a bit at the occasions when a person attends one, picks up a superficial idea of something new, and then "applies" it in her or his practice.

Every academic program, every scholarly journal, and every clinical training program is in the business of trying to influence quality and direction of professional work. The realistic questions may have to do mostly with which kinds of influence will be most successful and in which directions.

On the other hand, if attempts to influence large social systems were already well understood and therefore readily effective, there would be less reason to criticize the present effectiveness of social science. It is possible that few of the people attempting to influence professional work know exactly how to achieve the results intended. Certainly, I do not.

Few of the thoughts expressed here are unique. There is no decisive reason to think that my expressing them gives them any special force. Even if some of the more concrete suggestions made here were actually implemented, the consequences in terms of quality could turn out to be slight or quite different than anticipated.

Ultimately, I return to the attitude expressed in the chapter on minimal therapy. If even bits and pieces of social science and socially oriented therapy are not in some sense "ready" for some slight movement in the directions suggested in this book, movement will not occur. If any change does happen, perhaps in the attitudes of a few people, I will be able to flatter myself that I have had a small contribution to make as one of perhaps many advisory midwives. The more sober thought is that any change would have happened anyway and that this work is best regarded as only a minor expression of a social system that is currently ruminating about change. There are any number of ways that this work can be regarded. Perhaps it is the latest expression of whatever my family has been up to. Perhaps it is best regarded as someone's middle-aged craziness. Even if all these things are true, perhaps there is still some sense in regarding these essays as a collection of ideas, one or two of which might be of interest. Point of view is important.

References

Bell, Richard Q. (1968). A reinterpretation of the direction of effects in studies of socialization. *Psychological Review, 75*, 81-95.

Berman, Eric. (1973). *Scapegoat.* Ann Arbor: University of Michigan Press.

Bridgman, Percy. (1927). *The logic of modern physics.* New York: Macmillan.

Burgess, Anthony. (1963). *A clockwork orange.* New York: W.W. Norton.

Capellanus, Andreus. (1959). *The art of courtly love.* (J. D. Parry, Trans.). New York: Frederick Unger.

Cervantes, Saavedra Miguel de. (1949). *Don Quixote de la Mancha* (S. Putman, Ed. and Trans.). New York: Viking Press. (Original work published 1605, 1611)

Dector, Midge. (1972). *The new chastity and other arguments against women's liberation.* New York: Coward McCann and Geohegan.

De Rougemont, Denis. (1956). *Love in the Western world.* New York: Pantheon.

Doherty, W. J., McCabe, P., & Ryder, Robert G. (1978). Marriage encounter: A critical appraisal. *Journal of Marriage and Family Counseling, 4*, 99-107.

Dray, William. (1962). Some causal accounts of the American Civil War. *Daedalus, 19*, 578-598.

Driscoll, Richard, Davis, Keith, & Lipetz, Martin E. (1972). The Romeo and Juliet effect. *Journal of Personality and Social Psychology, 24*, 1-10.

Freud, Sigmund. (1962). Group psychology and the analysis of the ego. In *The major works of Sigmund Freud.* Chicago: Encyclopaedia Britannica. (Originally published in 1921)

Gergen, Kenneth J. (1982). *Toward transformation in social knowledge.* New York: Springer-Verlag.

Goffman, Erving. (1969). *Strategic interaction.* Philadelphia: University of Pennsylvania Press.

Goodrich, D. W., & Boomer, D. S. (1963). Experimental assessment of modes of conflict resolution. *Family Process, 2*, 15-24.

Gould, Thomas. (1963). *Platonic love.* London: Routledge and Kegan Paul.

Hathaway, Stark R., & McKinley, John C. (1951). *The Minnesota multiphasic personality inventory manual* (rev. ed.). New York: Psychological Corporation.

Henry, Jules. (1965). *Pathways to madness.* New York: Random House.

Hepworth, Jeri, Ryder, Robert G., & Dreyer, Albert S. (1984). The effects of parental loss on the formation of intimate relationships. *Journal of Marriage and Family Therapy, 10*, 73-82.

Hofstader, D. R. (1980). *Gödel, Escher, and Bach: An eternal braid.* New York: Vintage.

Hull, Clark L. (1933). *Hypnosis and suggestibility: An experimental approach.* New York: Appleton-Century-Crofts.

Jacobson, Gary, & Ryder, Robert G. (1969). Parental loss and some characteristics of the early marriage relation. *Orthopsychiatry, 39,* 779-787.

Kaiser, Hellmuth. (1965). *Effective psychotherapy.* New York: Free Press.

Kuhn, Thomas S. (1970). *The structure of scientific revolutions* (2nd ed.). Chicago: University Press.

Lee, John A. (1976). *The colors of love.* Englewood Cliffs, NJ: Prentice-Hall.

Locke, H. J., & Wallace, K. M. (1959). Short marital adjustment prediction tests: Their reliability and validity. *Marriage and Family Living, 21,* 251-255.

Martin, Peter, & Bird, H. Waldo. (1962). One type of the "in-search-of-a-mother" marital patterns. *Psychiatric Quarterly, 36,* 283-293.

Murstein, Bernard I. (Ed.). (1971). *Theories of attraction and love.* New York: Springer.

Roszak, Theodore, (1972). *Where the wasteland ends: Politics of transcendence in postindustrial society.* New York: Doubleday.

Rubin, Zick. (1970). Measurement of romantic love. *Journal of Personality and Social Psychology, 16,* 265-273.

Rychlak, Joseph F. (1977). *The psychology of rigorous humanism.* New York: Wiley.

Ryder, Robert G. (1966). The factualizing game: A sickness of psychological research. *Psychologist Report, 19,* 536-570.

Ryder, Robert G. (1972). What is power? Definitional considerations and some research considerations. *Science and Psychoanalysis, 20,* 36-52.

Ryder, Robert G. (1986). Professional's values in family assessment. *Counseling and Values, 30,* 24-34.

Ryder, Robert G., Kafka, John A., & Olson, David H. (1971). Separating and joining factors in courtship and early marriage. *American Journal of Orthopsychiatry,* 450-464.

Singer, Irving. (1966). *The nature of love: Plato to Luther.* New York: Random House.

Slater, Philip E. (1963). On social regression. *American Sociological Review, 28,* 339-364.

Sullivan, H. S. (1953). *The interpersonal theory of psychiatry.* New York: W.W. Norton.

Tessor, Abraham, & Paulhus, Delroy. Toward a causal model of love. *Journal of Personality and Social Psychology, 34,* 1095-1105.

Tharp, Roland G. (1963). Psychological patterning in marriage. *Psychological Bulletin, 60,* 97-117.

Wilcox, J. T. (1964). From is to ought via psychology. *Review of Metaphysics, 18,* 254-266.

Yerkes, R. M., & Dodson, J. D. (1908). The relation of strength of stimulus to rapidity of habit formation. *Journal of Comparative Neurology and Psychology, 18,* 459-482.

ABOUT THE AUTHOR

Robert G. Ryder is Dean of Family Studies at the University of Connecticut. Before coming to Connecticut in 1974, he was Chief of the Section on Family Development at the National Institute of Mental Health, in which he had served since 1961 with such colleagues as Wells Goodrich, Harold Raush, Richard Bell, Howard Moss, and Mary Waldrop. His graduate training in psychology was under Edward Bordin at the University of Michigan. Ryder's work has been concerned primarily with marriage and other intimate relationships. He is a member of the American Psychological Association, the National Conference on Family Relations, the Association of Sex Educators, Counselors and Therapists, and the American Family Therapy Association. He is a Fellow in the American Association for Marriage and Family Therapy, and is a board member and past president of the Groves Conference on Marriage and the Family. He is on the editorial boards of the *Journal of Marriage and Family Therapy*, the *Journal of Family Issues*, and *Family Process*, and is on the board of directors of *Family Process*. Ryder has been active as a researcher, administrator, therapist, and teacher of therapists.

NOTES

NOTES

NOTES